what the hell are they trying to prove, martha?

what the hell are they

richard atcheson

a

wary

convert's

report

on

the

new

self-expression

in

america

today

trying to prove, martha?

the John Day company

new york

The John Day Company, 257 Park Avenue South, New York, N.Y. 10010
an Intext publisher

Published on the same day in Canada by Longmans Canada Limited

Library of Congress Catalogue Card Number: 74-107205
Printed in the United States of America
Designed by the Etheredges

for jean

contents

and
I am
waiting
for
lovers
and
weepers
to
lie
down
together
again
in
a
new
rebirth
of
wonder
LAWRENCE FERLINGHETTI

introduction: still alive at thirty-five

i confess that whatever the titles listed in the table of contents, this book is mostly about me, and I would like to explain why that has to be. On the face, it is a collection of articles about a wide spectrum of improbable places and events. Most of these articles were published in *Holiday* magazine over the last few years, and the arrangement is almost entirely chronological, though the pieces collected here are only a fraction of my total output for *Holiday*.

In some cases they are not what I consider to represent the best of my articles—but in every case they tell quite a lot about what has been happening on the perimeters of our society in recent years, and they show, in the development and growth which I think is implicit in them, even more about what has happened to me—as a writer and, more pertinently, as a human being.

I started out in journalism as a reporter for the *Chicago Daily News*. I learned some good lessons there, and many painful ones—and a few ridiculous ones, which it has taken me many years to unlearn. Principal among these is the long-standing rule of journalistic objectivity, which is another way of saying that the writer is never to be present in his story, and certainly never to appear to *feel* anything. That rule runs contrary to the human experience, of course —so bluntly against the surge of human emotion that it is something of a miracle that the rule has been honored by so many journalists for so many years. It also helps to explain, I think, why so many newspapermen and magazine writers are hopeless drunks. In any event, there will always be people who can play that kind of newspaper game; perhaps that fact is a living tribute to the miracle.

But I can't play that game any more—and as our society opens, and as I attend professionally upon its amazing debut, I am finding fewer and fewer necessities to lie, to cover up, or to disappear utterly from the lines I write. In a time when the mere presence of a TV cameraman incites events and creates news, it is time for the inconspicuous writer to admit that he, too, is really there.

The consequences of that admission, for the nonfiction

writer, are risky. He becomes, for the first time, vulnerable—as liable to criticism, as open to the charge of exhibitionism, as any novelist or poet. But novelists and poets have always known that personal danger comes with their territory. The nonfiction writer has to run the gantlet without much psychic preparation—and I confess that it's scary out there without any clothes on.

But better. Better for the writer, God knows, and better for the general dissemination of information, and infinitely more supportive of some real honesty in the ongoing chronicle of the human experience.

It took me a long time to come to this position, which should be abundantly clear from the arrangement of these articles, and the character of each. The story of Reston, the new town, leads the book because it marks the point at which I first began to realize that there was in the country a new and restless trend toward the practical exploration of fresh ideas. There was an appetite suddenly for risk and adventure, massive change, which I hadn't even suspected before. I fell in love with Reston, and got so excited about the shape of the new community that I spoke of getting a job in Washington, just so I could live with my family in the new town. But you won't find much of that flaming enthusiasm in the piece. For the most part, it is a dry, competent exposition of the salient facts of Reston—just the sort of uninvolved essay that *Holiday* was running that year, and had run for twenty years before it.

In writing about Old Town in Chicago, I let more of my feelings seep in. I had lived there, I had married there, it was important to me—and I thought I'd try a more personal involvement in the text and see if my editors would print it. Somewhat to my surprise, they did, and more or less as I had written it.

The Bennington piece was harder. As you will discover nowhere in the article, the Bennington girls frightened me. They were apparently smarter than I was, much more adventurous, and worse—they seemed to know something or intuit something about life that I couldn't figure out. In terribly important ways they were free—I said as much in the lead paragraphs of the piece, but I still didn't understand what it was they knew that I didn't.

The Atlantic City piece represents, for me, the first giant step into personal journalism. It is about what happened to me and mine, and really, except as those events illumine the subject, that is *all* it's about. However, there is by that act more of a sense of place in the piece than could possibly exist in a carefully sterile, impersonal descriptive essay. I began to see that I did not want simply to tell people about other people and other places; I wanted to bring my reader with me, onto the plane, into the theater, and if need be, under the table. That meant, as in ordinary human relationships, that I had to be honest first with myself, in order to convey not only the precise nature of the events but the emotional realities within which I perceived them.

Esalen was the turning point. My feeble concern about honest and involved prose came smack up against the incontrovertible fact that I was a liar, and a liar who always lied first and best to himself. I brooded for many weeks on the few choices I had. To continue to write in my old, constipated style was clearly impossible. Give up writing? I didn't think I could. The only thing to do, I felt, was to try to write really straight, to eliminate the bullshit, to tell the truth as I saw and felt it.

The rest of the pieces show the results of the effort. Some work better than others, and there are times when I wish there were no first-person pronoun in the language. But what I have to say is as honest as I can manage to be, and I never hide my bias. This way, people who dislike me can do so for perfectly obvious reasons.

They would be, I suppose, the same people who will dislike the developments I have written about, the manifestations of a freer and more expressive society than we have known before in this country. I think freedom is a terrifying thing, but I find the climate so intoxicating that I can contemplate, with some calm, the dues that must be paid in fear, anxiety, and pain. Cheap, anytime, at twice the price.

When I was an undergraduate at Princeton in 1956, I wrote a column for the *Alumni Weekly* called "On the Campus." Cramped little weevil of a budding journalist, careful cropped Princetonian though I was, I wrote something at some point that infuriated masses of alumni, and they wrote in a flurry of letters to the editor, demanding that I be discharged. One protester, a dentist in a small New Jersey town, wrote that I was obviously a Communist or a crypto-Communist, and he predicted that I would commit suicide before I was thirty-five.

That was, of course, an extraordinary wish to project upon any boy not yet twenty-one, but I was glad to have the letter and have kept it these many years. It was, you see, the first sign I'd had that I could touch someone else by writing—and I have never turned back. I have, however, turned thirty-five.

when I was a child, I was frightened by a planned community—Pullman Village, on the far South Side of Chicago—and I have been suspicious of imposed order and neatness ever since. Pullman Village was built in the late nineteenth century by George Pullman, the railroad-car king, for obligatory use by his factory workers. It was praised in those days as a spectacular exercise in enlightened philanthropy, and it is conceivable that the old man was well intentioned. But it had grown old and tatty long before I saw it, in 1950, and the hopeless decay of the place only underlined the basic wretchedness of the idea and the improbability that it could ever have been a happy place for anyone to live in. I gaped at the grim rows of identical, mean little cottages in red brick, and the sad efforts of occupants to assert individuality—a hedge here, an electric-blue trim there. I noted the ramshackle frame room added onto almost every cottage, crowding each narrow back yard—added not to provide family living space but accommodation for a boarder, to help make ends meet. And always the sightless great walls of the factory closed out the north end of each dreary street. I went away with the youthful conviction that even chaos had to be better.

But lately I have been poking around Reston, Virginia, another planned community, and I have had to change my mind. Reston is a new town, grown up from scratch out of a country field. There are more than eighty new-town projects in various stages of development in the United States at this moment, but so far Reston is the only one you can see and touch, and it is worth the experience. It is beautiful and it is bizarre. And as few buildings and landscapes ever are, it is full of excitement and risk.

Reston is a dream turned into mortar by Robert E. Simon, a New York real estate entrepreneur who used to own Carnegie Hall and still owns or controls millions of dollars' worth of real estate all over the country. In 1960 he bought 7,150 acres of wooded countryside twenty-three miles from Washington, D.C., in the Virginia hunt country, and with the backing principally of the Gulf Oil Corporation, immediately began to transform the bucolic landscape into a minutely planned community that would ultimately number seventy thousand people. There is in the exercise of Simon's grand design a disturbing echo of Shaw's character in *Major Barbara,* Sir Andrew Undershaft, munitions magnate, who likewise aspired to "organize civilization," and this troubles some critics. The attitudes of the two men, one real, one fictional, are strikingly similar. But the differences are that Simon does not make bombs, only houses, and that his plan is far superior to the best that Shaw could dream up in 1905.

For the purposes of his play, Shaw borrowed the garden-city concept first proposed by Ebenezer Howard, an English inventor, in 1898. Howard simply spoke up for fresh new towns in the countryside, supported by their own industry, to take the strain off the great impacted industrial centers. Letchworth, the first garden city to grow out of Howard's proposal, was being built outside London and was attracting widespread interest and controversy while Shaw was writing *Major Barbara.* Of course, Shaw put a special gloss on the basic new-town idea by adding to Undershaft's complex "The Meeting Place of All the Religions," a great square of churches and temples to all gods, in architecture of every description. Robert Simon's master plan for Reston also puts a high gloss on the original garden-city concept, but it is much more practical and considerably more fetching.

The first Reston cluster, Lake Anne Village, is focused on a long man-made lake with a docile, canallike boat basin at one end and a wide body of water at the other. Subsequent clusters, each for about ten thousand residents, will have different themes (Lake Anne is the only lake contemplated). The second cluster will be gathered around a vast riding barn and stables. The barn is up, the horses are at home, and the bridle paths are already there, a built-in feature of horse-loving Fairfax County. The rest is woods, but Simon confidently asserts that it will be a rustic total environment, with homes, shops, schools, and all, in fairly short order. It will also be somewhat more modest than Lake Anne Village.

Lake Anne Village had to be spectacularly lavish in every detail in order to attract the publicity Reston needs to put itself over. Simon's money rides on the widest possible acceptance of the new-town idea generally, and of Reston specifically, for he is selling a concept that runs directly against American home-buying tastes established after World War II—split-level suburbia, automobile-dependent, every house smack in the middle of a quarter-acre "estate" —all the features that made the bulldozer king of the land and achieved low population density at the cost of the "good life" that buyers thought they were getting. Lake Anne Village, and theoretically all of Reston, turns these trends upside down by eliminating private lawns, pulling houses into attached rows or clusters, and providing all the services and amenities, in advance, that other kinds of residential development do without for years until the tax base is strong enough to support them. The most impressive aspect of Lake Anne Village is that it is all already *there,* ready for the appraisal of prospective buyers and publicists of good will. On the debit side is the fact that those same amenities—the lake, the sweeping lawns and wooded knolls and hollows, the playgrounds, pools, tennis courts and golf course, the shops and services installed and functioning, the central air-conditioning system that serves the whole village—have added some six hundred dollars to the price of every house in the place.

Another obviously costly element of Lake Anne Village is the high quality of its design. There are many different kinds of houses and apartments in the village, designed by three architectural firms in distinctive styles. All of them are essentially contemporary, extremely handsome, and not in the least hokey. At the butt end of Lake Anne, accessible from the country road it borders, is Washington Plaza, the commercial center of the village, distinctly urban in character, with shops and clubrooms and a saloon all housed in the U-shaped building that enfolds the plaza. Over the shops are apartments with big windows and balconies, and from one end of the plaza a row of townhouses runs along the lakeside at water's edge. Across the open end of the plaza are more townhouses and the sixteen-story apartment house which, in these modern times, performs the eye-lifting duties once assigned to the church spire.

These buildings, all designed by the New York firm of Whittlesey and Conklin, are of concrete and dark-brown brick, and they seem rough-edged and rugged. There is a suggestion of crenelation in the roof outlines that is almost medieval, certainly severe—but, in the soft environment of leafy woods and dreaming lake, precisely right. The open walkways (this area is closed to cars) and wide pavements are punctuated by the playful sculptures of Gonzalo Fonseca, who designed them with children in mind. There is a "sun boat" set in the pavement, there are mazes and odd, climbable structures of concrete, and, at the water's edge, an unaccountable construction that could be the prow of a great, landlocked ship, or perhaps a pompous pulpit from which to preach to the fishes.

Around a bend and over a footbridge are the pastel row houses of Chloethiel Smith, whose work here strangely echoes both Georgetown and Portofino. Beyond them, off the lake, are the assertively modern townhouse clusters of Washington architect Charles M. Goodman. Set into a hillside, they are full of surprises—unexpected courts and patios, second-floor entrances, overpass footpaths—evoking a tucked-away, nook-and-cranny feeling in what might have been just routine space.

On the whole, the major accomplishment of all three architectural efforts is that they innovate, delight the eye, and respect and—who ever heard of such a thing before?— *enhance* the natural landscape. Because these designs are so extraordinary and so successful, they let early residents of Lake Anne Village in on something exciting, and that in itself is a sales point. Buyers can expect to have front-row seats for one of the most death-defying exhibitions of wire-walking ever attempted in the history of real estate, as Robert Simon inches forward toward the total Reston, the total environment.

Reston is not meant to be exclusively a commuting exurb for Washington workers but, in the future, a self-supporting civic entity. The master plan allots 14 percent of the total acreage to industrial and business development, and Reston's sales staff is aimed full tilt at likely corporate customers. The idea is that one day as many as 60 percent of Reston's breadwinners can live and work and play in contiguous areas, without having to fragment their lives, and those of their families, by traveling long distances to and from their jobs. The success of Reston depends heavily on industry's recognition that the combined features of an industrial park and a residential park are just what business ordered. The prospects look good. Several firms have already located there or have committed themselves to do so, either in an industrial quadrangle built by Simon or in buildings of their own. Senior among these is the distillery of two popular bourbon whiskeys, Virginia Gentleman and Fairfax, which was there when Simon bought the land from the distillery owners, known locally as the Bowman family of Fairfax County. So the distillery endures in this new environment, as do the Bowmans, who sold the acreage but retained their homes.

Reston is, of course, prepared to accommodate its industrial buyers amply. It is no accident, for example, that the industrial park borders on a beautiful eighteen-hole golf course.

Nor is it any accident that large chunks of Reston's outer acreage have been sold or otherwise assigned to speculators for independent housing developments—some good, some not so good, none really ghastly, but none up to the unusual standards set by Lake Anne Village. These back-acre pockets have nothing of the dominant Reston image about them. They look like most other real estate speculations. Back, in other words, to a house in the middle of every lot, and every lot as narrow as the buyer will endure. The woods are still there, and still look good, but the houses, jammed up on each other, too large and too showy for their sites, are not much of a complement to the trees.

Though the Reston management retains a certain amount of aesthetic control over these developers, they have occasionally allowed more latitude than proved wise in the end. For example, though Fairfax County is slightly north of Washington, old traditions die hard, and it is still true that in Virginia you can sell almost any kind of box if you stick a few pillars out in front and call it Tara. Secure in this sure-fire gambit, a couple of the speculators have created some stylistic inconsistencies as jarring as anything you can find in the cheapest developments. But the presence of a few porticos in ante-bellum style does give the lie to disgruntled observers of Reston who complain that you can't achieve personal expression in such a totalitarian system.

As one Washingtonian put it, "If I want to grow a rose, I want to grow a goddamn rose." He was referring to the fact that, in Lake Anne Village, there are a number of things you may not do, as articulated by the management. You might, perhaps, grow a rose—preferably in a pot, possibly even along the edge of your house—but grounds keeping is organized collectively, by residential cluster, since the lawns and general landscaping are shared in common. Simon leaves these details to the residents in the cluster, but a Reston grounds-keeping crew is available and may be retained. Moreover, you may not hang wash on a line outside your house, because in the view of the Reston management, wash on a line is untidy. But Simon has thoughtfully provided outlets in every basement for washer and dryer.

You may not wish to consort with your neighbors, in which case you should not buy in Reston in the first place, since you are obliged to shop in the same stores with them, visit the same library, send your children to the same schools, drink at the same bar, and tread the same green-sward at all times. But you must do all these things in almost any other neighborhood, too, and it will probably not have outdoor swimming pools and tennis courts close at hand. And Simon has arranged that these shall be private amenities, clubs for membership only. So if you are reluctant to consort with your neighbors, you can never claim that you were forced into togetherness with them by being pushed into an open pool.

Though Reston is obviously not for everybody, neither is New York or Levittown, and I have little time for curmudgeons who distrust planning even when it works. After all, Reston is a far cry from Pullman Village. Similar communities have flourished in Europe, and they are not dull centers for mindless automatons. Tapiola, a new town in Finland, has even achieved integration of income groups (unheard of and desperately feared in most of this country) by maintaining common standards of good design in all housing. Your next-door neighbor may pay twice as much for his house as you pay for yours, but his greater space or convenience will not be embarrassingly apparent because your house looks as fine as his. Simon has identical ambitions for Reston, and with any luck he will ultimately realize them.

I saw Reston for the first time on a winter weekend evening, at twilight. No lights were showing, and the rugged rear of Washington Plaza loomed black and forbidding against the sky. But people were stumbling through a dark passage into the plaza, over the flotsam of workers' equipment, piles of sand, and cinder block. I crunched along after them, and just as I turned into the plaza, the first crisp notes of a trumpet voluntary cut the cold night air. I had walked in on Reston's first "cultural event," a concert by a brass choir. Some two hundred people, perhaps three-fourths of them children, had bundled up for the occasion and were huddled together enjoying the music. The children conducted for the fun of it, or sang along, and even the bad numbers got a lot of applause—but the biggest hit was a performance by coach horns. The musicians climbed up on the balconies over the unfinished shops and stores and played antiphonally over our heads. The vaguely crenelated rooftops of the enclosing court rang with the sound, and it was very exciting and hopeful. I was reminded that besides the groups of professional architects and city planners who constantly roam through Reston on guided tours, a curiously appropriate crowd had come that week. The Reston *Report,* a newsletter, had listed them as "an Episcopal Sunday-school class, viewing Reston during its study of the Kingdom of God on earth."

Alas, an earthly paradise did not rise up. Reston never quite caught on with buyers—not, at least, in the numbers Simon needed to support continued growth—and in the end control passed into the hands of far less visionary committees. The development of Reston has entered upon its dowdier, lackluster days, and the great dream will remain, forever, just that. And as that dream roams rootless through the collective unconscious, I hope it tarries now and then to trouble the sleep of the practical money men who would not see it through to concrete completion.

new life in old town

there is a little piece of Chicago real estate, west of Lincoln Park, that is the pride of urban conservationists and the despair of bulldozers. It is a community widely known as Old Town, a label pinned on it by an itinerant publicist but adequate enough as labels go. Old Town is probably the most amusing neighborhood in the country; certainly the most entertaining one ever to outsmart urban renewal. Nobody ever had to lie down in the street for Old Town, either. Its friends and lovers didn't picket for it;

they improved it. So when the Chicago Plan Commission took a suspicious look, some years ago, they found a neighborhood ripe for conservation instead of demolition. As part of a larger urban renewal scheme, Old Town will be altered slightly in the next few years—a widened avenue here, a closed mall there—but none of the projected changes will shatter the character of its streets or the sense of community which animates its people.

It is surprising that Old Town should have that sense of community. Its past is chequered with disasters, its residents are a mix of Germans, Irish, Italians, Negroes, Hungarians, Puerto Ricans, Mexicans, Syrians, Greeks, Japanese, Appalachian whites, and WASPS, and its architecture a kaleidoscope of Victorian overindulgence and dyspepsia. Old Town is full of weekend bohemians, precocious children, bawdy beer parlors, hanging gardens, and stone Cupids. It spawns improvement and betterment associations faster than a hot knife cuts butter, and they flail away at each other right and left, seized with a common panic born of Old Town's swift and dizzying rise from slum tattiness to urban stardom. Wells Street, Old Town's main drag, has undergone an even more accelerated elevation. Five years ago it was a dowdy old charlady of a street, lined with frame boardinghouses and taxi garages. Today it's a shameless hussy, a twinkly, tinselly Great White Way of crazy shops and nutty bars, a commercial area now turning over a multimillion-dollar yearly retail gross where six years ago you could walk blocks without encountering anybody but muggers. And Old Town, which did not count on all this fame and notoriety as part of the residential Good Life, is plainly scared to death. Some of Old Town's lovers would really rather have the muggers back.

Three groups seem to describe the activist landscape. The Old Town Triangle Association is composed of the old-timers and hold-the-liners. Their organization is almost wholly responsible for the fact that there is an Old Town to fight over in 1967, and by service and longevity alone they deserve a respectful hearing. Then there's the Old Wells Association, a self-help blood brotherhood of Wells Street merchants dominated by many of the original shoe-string shopkeepers who started the whole money thing by, to their astonishment, making a lot of it in a hurry. The third group is the Old Town Chamber of Commerce. A lot of the newest money being poured into the area is not liked by the somewhat older money. So the Chamber of Commerce is the improvement association that new money made. Members of the Chamber tend to think that the Old Wells people are unwashed amateurs, probably nuts. The Old Wells people think of the Chamber as a sort of Cosa Nostra. The Triangle people cry a pox on both their houses and wish they would all go away, taking their twenty-five thousand tourists a night with them. It was not for this, they say, that they labored so hard for so many years.

The old-timers cannot see that a tourist-shy Old Town, set in amber, would not suit them either, and that the explosions of phenomenal growth, execrable taste, and monumental bad temper are all essential to the quality of Old Town's life style. The place is pretty, yes, and popular. But its greatest strength is that it constantly vibrates with kinetic energy. Old Town is full of conflict, full of life, a sometimes maddening but always exciting place to live. It may be, in fact, depending on one's proclivities in such matters, the nicest place in the world.

I used to think so, anyway. My wife and I had our first apartment in Old Town, in a red-brick Victorian house redesigned by a Japanese architect, and I am awash with sentiment every time I think of it. Also venality. I had lived in New York, she in San Francisco, and we both knew we could never have anything like *this* in either polar city. For not very much money, we had a skating rink of polished floor space, high white walls, rooms flooded with sunlight, a sybaritic bathroom with slatted ceiling, *four* tiny bedrooms, and a brick-walled garden at the back. We also had an Oriental Santa Claus for a landlord, some interestingly emotional but not pushy neighbors, charming, tree-lined streets to walk in, and a fifteen-minute bus ride to the Loop. In summer you put on your bathing suit and walked through Lincoln Park to the beach in a matter of minutes. Summer or winter, on a thirsty evening, the Twin Anchors and the Old Town Ale House comprised the circuit of local night life. Scratch a nubby sweater or a pair of Levi's in either place and you'd discover a municipal bond salesman in hiding from LaSalle Street respectability, but those joints always *looked* racy enough, and we bought our own Bohemia with a twenty-five-cent stein of lager.

We knew people who had spent thousands of dollars on décor and wouldn't let you sit on certain chairs. We knew others, more like ourselves, who furnished their apartments from the Salvation Army exclusively, and you couldn't sit on some of those chairs, either. We even knew some people who turned the whole ground floor of their classic old house into a mad aviary, with birds flying all over the place and perching indiscriminately on tree limbs and guests. It was that kind of place. Most of it still is.

It is important to stress, however, that there is no such legal entity as Old Town. Old Town is where you make it. The Triangle people insist that it's only in the "triangle," an accident of streets that, seen from the air, would seem to suggest a sort of wobbly arrowhead pointing north. Wells Street could be said to form the shaft of our fictional arrow, an off-center shaft to be sure, but one running zip-zap up from the south and penetrating the triangle clear through. Old Town really means just patterned, textured, informal living in a pleasant urban environment. You can do it to the west and north of the triangle, and even here and there off the shaft of Wells Street. People have been doing it there for years.

But quite another sort of life exists in and on the fringes of Old Town, and there are historic sites nearby that only a tough old city like Chicago could provide. The garage where the St. Valentine's Day massacre occurred is just a few blocks from the triangle. So is the Biograph Theater, where Dillinger was gunned down, and a venerable telephone pole in the alley still bears the scars. Paddy Bauler, interminable and indestructible alderman of the 43rd Ward, of which Old Town is a part, still politicks on North Avenue, the southern boundary of the triangle, though his Deluxe Gardens tavern, with its famous, smoke-filled backroom, closed as a saloon in 1960. Paddy put his seal on the city's history some years ago when he remarked, "Chicago ain't ready for reform." These days, confronted with a ward gone at least partially wild, he tries to keep up with the times. "Keep it quaint," he gamely urges.

Strangely, what is now Old Town has always been sort of quaint, even before the Great Fire of 1871. Before the Civil War, when it was outside the city limits, marked by North Avenue, the area was called the Cabbage Patch. That was, perhaps, because the German settlers who developed the area grew cabbages. Or it was just a denigrating thing for WASPs to say about all those German farmers out north, with their notorious appetite for cabbage. When the area was annexed in 1851, it was known as North Town, still solidly and very obviously German. Nor could the great conflagration of October 8, 1871, burn away the ethnic configurations that the city had already assumed. The fire traveled south to north in a wide swath, burning every building in North Town to the ground, except for the walls of St. Michael's Church, a brand-new stone structure built to serve the German populace. Back they came, doggedly, to rebuild their church and community, and set their mark architecturally on all the streets of Old Town. The ubiquitous high cottages, little houses raised a full flight off the ground, came into being out of German village custom, which demands that the ground level be given over to storage and tacking and god knows what homely purposes, while decent family living could be conducted only on the second floor and above.

Three thousand "relief cottages," flimsy frame outfits, were built by the city in Old Town after the fire, but only one or two survive. Most were speedily replaced by the high frame cottages and, through the prosperous years that followed, wilder and more elaborate styles of housing in frame, brick, stone, and plaster. The German builders were no architects; they were just professional craftsmen practicing riotous eclecticism at a time when just about anything went. The carpenters and masons delighted in pursuing little personal details; they showed off outrageously on every cornice and stair railing and plaster ceiling they touched. Their legacy is a complex of fanciful dwellings, made with love and all but sealed with a kiss. They liked Gothic pointed windows, Renaissance pilasters, mansard roofs, swooping, looping eaves and Bessarabian balconies, and they liked them all mixed up together on the same house. So what you get today in the short, stop-and-start streets of Old Town is a rich architectural goulash that somehow turns out to be exactly to taste. The pleasant effect is heighened, of course, by the agreeable human scale of the neighborhood—the streets are narrow, random rows, popping into each other by surprise here and there, turning unexpectedly into tiny mews streets or opening into broader thoroughfares. But the grid pattern is almost completely absent, nothing is ever predictable or routine, and there is a kind of silly, lovely elegance about it all.

At any odds, one of the most charming areas in Old Town is Crilly Court, which dates from 1877. Daniel Crilly, a wealthy South Side contractor (in the days after the fire, any contractor had to get wealthy), bought a full city block in the triangle, cut a north–south street through it, and filled it with very stylish row houses and four large apartment houses. A sentimentalist, Crilly named the four large buildings after his four children, and today you can still live in Isabelle, Oliver, Erminnie, or Edgar. I think I would prefer Erminnie for the sheer novelty of it. The houses back up on one another to form a protected court, and most of the apartments give onto balconies and adjoin and overlook each other in a most neighborly way. Some of the tenants have grown up great jungles of flowering creeper and the balconies are festooned with it, rollicking and cascading up and down and around. This gloss of creeper tells a lot about the people who live in Old Town. Nice as they are, Isabelle, Oliver, Erminnie, and Edgar are not particularly distinguished buildings. But the people who live in them have made them memorable.

A number of Chicago's resident intellectual lights live in Crilly Court today, but none of them is so colorful as an earlier resident, George K. Spoor. Spoor provided the "S" part of the Essanay Film Company, which thrived on early Westerns when Hollywood really was a cabbage patch. They went in for Westerns mostly because the "A" in Essanay was Bronco Billy Anderson, a big star in those days. They also went in for comedy, and the first Keystone Cop on film chased his first bandit down Eugenie Street and into Crilly Court. It is said that parties given in Crilly Court by Spoor and Bronco Billy were Really Something.

Very gradually, Old Town began to suffer from the attrition which inevitably affected the German community as some of them got richer and began to prefer the suburbs. A hard core of German settlers' descendants is still there, however, and the pretentious old Germania Club still stands on Clark Street as a bastion of traditional *Gemütlichkeit*. When the club celebrated its hundredth anniversary, in 1965, its membership was addressed by a West German diplomat who said, *"Lassen Sie mich Ihnen zu Beginn von Herzen Glück wünschen zu dem 100. Geburtstage des Germania Clubs und Ihnen auch für die Zukunft wünschen, dass der Club weiter blühen und gedeihen möge"*—and unless Mayor Daley was there, there couldn't have been a soul in the room who needed a translation.

During the 1920's and 1930's, Old Town fell on really evil days. Many old-timers remained, but money was scarce, upkeep wasn't cheap, and the triangle and all the streets around it developed a discouragingly seedy look. It wasn't a shambles, and it took inside its borders many of the ethnic elements who now make its population so interestingly varied, but it was generally neglected and started to look dangerously like too much of Chicago still looks—straight, middle-class, and indifferent. Curiously, it took World War II to rally the populace to a new awareness of its environment and the special qualities it had, more in potential than in reality. In fact, the very concept of the triangle was imposed by a civil defense map, the triangle of streets becoming a city unit. People rushed into the streets in tin hats as block wardens or as victory garden boosters, and they came to think of their triangle as the Triangle. In 1948, having exchanged their tin hats for paint pots and rollers, the activist elements formed the Old Town Triangle Association, with a lawyer named James K. Beverly as first president. Beverly was an obvious choice for leadership. In 1940 he had bought and restored a row of once elegant houses on Wisconsin Avenue, demonstrating a confidence in the area that had not been seen for years.

Two years later, the association staged its first Art Fair, directly on the heels of Clean-up Week. The members had done a lot of sprucing up in the meantime, they had become aware that a number of Chicago painters and sculptors and artsy-craftsy types who did beadwork and leather stitching had lived in and around the triangle for a while, and they wanted to raise money for a local boys' club. So on a June weekend they closed off a couple of streets, got the local talents to set up stalls to sell their work from, and invited the public. And they were swamped. True, some of the beadwork was fantastically ugly. And some of the painters and sculptors weren't up to much either. But the ambiance was terrific. The tourists came in droves, strolled in the streets, had a beer at a streetside stand, maybe even bought a painting. And the Old Town Triangle Association, for all they may rue it today, had set the pattern for years to come. Old Town became Chicago's instant Bohemia, a whitewashed, tree-lined Greenwich Village, vaguely threatening but mostly innocent. In the years following, the local churches got in on the act. The Midwest Buddhist Church, right in the middle of Old Town, began dispensing chicken teriyaki dinners to all comers. The ladies at St. James's Church dispensed good, home-cooked German meals, filling and fattening. St. Michael's continued to dispense nothing but cold and forbidding Roman Catholicism, and the Moody Bible Church continued to dispense that old-time religion, but two out of four is not a bad participation record. The Art Fair, and through it all of Old Town, began to take on a reputation for providing reasonably safe thrills. It also became desirable, as it had never been before, to a wide spectrum of society. People walking through the streets during the fair could not miss the "in" quality of the event. They saw artists more or less lionized, if you can call a few yards of paintings hanging on somebody's picket fence lionization. They saw a beard-and-sandals set moving confidently around their streets, made much of by people in *chemises Lacoste*. Most important of all, they had a peek at the back gardens of Old Town, fancily got up in stone figures and fountains; Old Town residents coolly sipping gin and tonic on their balconies, idly resorting together in bermuda shorts, barefoot, almost disdainfully looking down on the madding throng below. And people were jealous. Why live stuffily in the far North in Mom and Dad's old apartment if we can be down here swinging? they asked themselves. So the rents began to climb, the powdering and painting of old houses intensified, the demand for service at the Twin Anchors and the Old Town Ale House got out of hand— and, willy-nilly, Wells Street was reborn.

It started in 1960, with a dumpy little joint called Moody's, a postcollege beer hall that caught on. Second City, Chicago's remarkable satirical cabaret, had already opened down the street, every night featuring the unknown likes of Barbara Harris and Alan Arkin, but it had spawned no new night-life development. Moody's, however, and an astonishing prescience, caused four law students to acquire an old storefront and start making it over into a new saloon. I remember walking down a dark, empty Wells Street one night with a bunch of friends, en route to Moody's, and we saw a group of young guys sawing away like crazy in this old storefront. We asked them what they were up to, Wells being that sort of street in those days, and they very agreeably told us they were building a new saloon and expected to make a pile of money. I also remember, bitterly, how we laughed as we continued on our way, pointing out to each other that Moody's already had all the business Wells Street could handle.

Chances R, which is what they called the place, was an overnight success. Gradually investing twenty-five thousand dollars in a décor that has been called "calculated dilapidation," the original four made a conspicuous bundle on good hamburgers, a mug's worth of beer, and as many peanuts as you could crack and eat. You were supposed to drop the shells on the floor and crunch around on them, for atmosphere. "Sensational!" everyone cried, and cracked and crunched in there, spending right and left, until the local smart money got the point. Since the success of Chances R there has been no turning back—for Wells Street or for Old Town as a whole.

These days, a walk north on Wells by daylight is a revelation in ugliness. Starting from Schiller, the first thing you notice is the big Dr. Scholl's factory on the west side of the street, with its big Dr. Scholl's sign. Beyond it, atop a building, a huge tin smokestack in the shape of a black ice cream cone rises oddly, the more odd for a sort of giant exhaust tube poking out the top of it. The buildings, a true hodgepodge here, look run-down, meanly thrown together at any height, sadly in need of attention. But Wells Street was always this ugly. What it now has, in addition, is the poky, bleached-out quality of any honky-tonk area, with yesterday's gay flags hanging soiled and tattered. By daylight, it's blowzy. And there is all that incredible filth in the streets—a Chicago specialty to be sure, filthy streets—but here, unparalleled, with parking tickets, old Kleenex, and a month's accumulation of effluvia banked against the buildings and impacting the gutters and drains. (A well-known collagist in Old Town once assembled a collage exclusively out of the trash that blew across her stoop in a month.) But Wells Street was always filthy.

Promptly at one o'clock every afternoon, the Skokie

matrons come to Wells Street. They're not all from Skokie, of course, but that is how they are called by the local antique and gallimaufry dealers, whose cluttered shops are their mecca. In among the innumerable drinking establishments (Mother Blues, a folk-rock joint; the Outhaus; the Plugged Nickel, quality jazz; the Crystal Pistol, bikini à go-go; the Snug, a piano bar decorated like a medieval torture chamber, with styrofoam chains and manacles on the walls) are equally innumerable potpourri shops, revving up every midday for this suburban invasion. The storekeepers need to have their wits about them. "Honest to God," said one, "you don't know what these women do. I find used Kleenex stuffed in with the fresh candy, cigarettes stubbed out in the fudge. And shoplifting! I have a rate of loss that would curl your hair." The merchant's lament is touching, and probably just, but he also has a record of earnings that would straighten my hair back again.

By late afternoon, the merchants are contending with the bus tours, great masses of people loping through with a quick right and left glance and a snatch and grab at some item of merchandise or other. The tourist buses go on cruising Wells Street and Old Town hour on hour, everybody goggling at everybody else with brash astonishment. The ogling sensation this last year has been the sudden excrescence of teeny-boppers on the street, literally hundreds of them day and night, thirteen years old and up, crowding in like their mothers from the suburbs for a taste of the sweet life. A tight circle of these kids are local drifters, in the sense that they never drift far from Maiden Lane, a new shopping arcade on Wells which features a Franksville hotdog stand out front. The local drifters are shaggy-haired boys and girls who wear beads and bell-bottoms, and they like to go barefoot on the rotten-dirty sidewalks and scandalize the passers-by. What each of the local drifters wears, five hundred Skokie teenagers want to buy, and then they all come down to Maiden Lane and stand around smoking Salems as if they were roll-your-own joints. Like most of Wells Street, the teeny-bopper element is largely borrowed and a little blue. It is also organized on a strictly first-name basis and its members are strictly inarticulate. "Long hair," they scream at each other in mock horror. "How disgusting!"

The police come along Wells with a chain of paddy wagons every now and then, stop at Maiden Lane, and arrest a hundred or so teenagers for such infractions as disorderly conduct or blocking the public way or breaking curfew. They load the kids into the wagons and then turn back to face a hundred or so more on the sidewalks and say they have room for more. The kids then scatter, but in ten minutes they are back where they were, scuffing up the white Colonial windowsills with their jackboots, patiently hanging on in hopes of they know not what. The windows of the shops in Maiden Lane stare back at them. Granny Goodfox, which purveys "boutique toys," gives them an eyeful of miniskirted Raggedy Annes and little tin soldiers. Stickers in the window of the Smuggler read, "THE GREEN HORNET IS A FAGGOT" and "MARY POPPINS IS A JUNKIE."

By night, lights ablaze and thousands of tourists and teenies and even some locals thronging the streets, Wells Street is in its glory. Many of the potpourri shops stay open; and, aware that they are themselves tourist attractions, some of them even charge admission. For twenty-five cents you get to wander in a wonderland of pine-scented pillows, candy canes, broken chandeliers, and felt beanbags. Far superior to this flotsam level is the Emporium, the best shop on the street. It's owned and operated by an anxious merchant named Ed Cordeira ("I sold the first Tiffany shade on this street for thirty-five dollars and was called a thief for it") in the best traditions of retail merchandising, and, in comparison with its shoddier neighbors, it stands out brightly on Wells. "Basically," says Cordeira, "we're the only people on the street, aside from Charlie's General Store, who spend any money on our windows. You know, changed every Monday. And I am out in front of this shop every morning with a hose, washing off the sidewalk." Cordeira is also the only merchant on Wells Street who seems to give a damn about the gas lamps that were expensively installed by the Old Wells Association a couple of years ago. Most of them are dirty, beat-up, fogged over, broken. Those in front of the Emporium are shiny, squeaky-clean, and bright, because Ed Cordeira is out there every morning polishing them up. "I guess nobody else really cares about it," he said. "You get the business whether you do anything or not. And the vandalism gets you down. Adult vandalism. People think this is their playground, their big fun playground."

When it is not vandalizing the merchants, the general public seeks its big fun in the restaurants and late-night joints. That Steak Joynt, a red-plush den that can handle only ninety-four at a sitting, has been grossing more than a million dollars a year for two years on account of its $150,000 décor and an unearned reputation for good eats. "Steak lovers!" its menu blurts in a spasm of narcissism. "Here's the moment you've dreamed about. Your opportunity to enjoy a prime steak prepared in the grand manner of the Victorian era." A comer is the newer Antonio's Steak House, where the atmosphere is all 1920's Chicago—just a little too golden yellow, a little too crystal-ornate—and all the waiters look like George Raft. The décor is more subtle and the food is better. The closest Wells Street comes to a plain old restaurant is probably the Soup's On, a very special outfit nonetheless. The Soup's On dispenses only soup, but good, rich, rib-sticking soup, dipped out of great copper pots. It's the best gustatory gimmick on the street.

Across and up the street from the Soup's On is the Sewer, an aptly named discothèque, and here the unwashed are sweatily frugging and monkeying around until all hours. Across the street from the Sewer, on Burton Place, is Le Bison, the grabbiest discothèque in Chicago but a private club and hard to enter without a recommendation at least. But Le Bison is worth the trouble. Its tiny dance floor features a two-story-high psychedelic light screen that oozes and pulsates with the beat of the music in at least fifty-seven different colors, its décor relies heavily on bunches of black balloons, and its clientele is as far out as Chicago ever gets. Ladies wrapped in silver foil, girls in transparent microskirts, and guys who shoot off cap pistols during the frenetic dancing are packed in there every night. The night I was there, one girl of a sadomasochistic persuasion carried her whip with her onto the dance floor and snapped it at fellow patrons in time with the music.

For real danger, there are joints up the street that could show that girl a thing or two. One or two have been closed by the police in the past year on such charges as beating up a patron (who turned out to be an off-duty cop) and suffering solicitation for prostitution on the premises. But genuine vice has never gotten much of a foothold in Old Town. Chicago seems to be able to tolerate almost any sort of bad action except prostitution, and the one bordello that ever opened shop on Wells Street was shuttered in two days. "They were stupid," a cop told me. "Advertising hot and cold running blondes on opening night. Everybody in town knew what was up."

Adjacent to some of the rougher bars is Old Town's newest shopping complex, a sort of Chicago-Arabian bazaar and souk called Piper's Alley. You see a monumental plastic "Tiffany" shade extruding into the street overhead, and beyond it, down an alley and into the bowels of a defunct bakery, a cobblestoned pathway chockablock with restaurants and boutiques and bars. It all cost more than three million dollars to install and, according to Rudy Schwartz, one of the masterminds, there is more More MORE to come. Schwartz used to be a merchandiser for Goldblatt's, and he knows merchandising. He and his partner have a piece of the action in every shop in Piper's Alley, in return for which they have provided a crazy, jumbled décor tailored to each shop's needs. Schwartz is glowingly confident. "Chicago is the jumpingest city in the country today," he says, almost jumping up and down himself, "and there's lots of money to be made on Wells Street for a long time . . . if you don't permit yourself to become a pig about it."

Rudy Schwartz is originally from New York. He talks like a New Yorker and he thinks like one. He came into Old Town with a lot of money, and some of the old-timers don't like him. But he knows what he's talking about. If Chicago is the jumpingest city in the country, Old Town is the jumpingest part of Chicago. And there is still room for everybody and everything—old character and hot times, dignity and dancing in the streets—so long as nobody ever gets to be a real pig about it.

bennington college:
we never danced on the grass

FIRST ALUMNA: We *never* danced on the grass. Never, *never!*
SECOND ALUMNA: Oh, Helen, you know we did. But only
for photographers.

the first time I ever saw a Bennington girl was
during a party weekend at Princeton. She burst through the
swinging doors of our club, threw her arms wide, and cried,
"Anybody want a date?" She explained that her date had
fallen into a drunken stupor at Ivy, and she wanted to know

why she should have traveled 250 miles down from Vermont just to sit and hold his head. We couldn't think of any reason, a friend of mine took her arm, and we went off party-hopping in a great group. The Bennington girl behaved very oddly, we thought. She would suddenly leap in the air, yelling "Catch me!" and if my friend didn't get there in time, she'd crash to the ground, laughing. She was perfectly sober, but she would pop into people's conversations with no introductions, snatch hats from people's heads, break into ex tempore modern dancing, and generally do exactly as she pleased with no regard for the social niceties we thought so important. Ultimately she ran off from us with a jazz musician from Trenton. It was the right thing for her to do. She was a free soul, and we weren't.

Twelve years later I met a Yale sophomore, as tweedy and pompous as only Ivy League sophomores can be, and he told me of his only blind date at Bennington. "Only time I ever went there," he said. "I found my date up in a tree, throwing apples at the moon." I have a lot more regard these days for throwing apples at the moon than I did when I was nineteen, and after investigation of the premises, I am happy to confirm the Yalie's report that Bennington is still supporting that kind of unself-conscious joy in its students. No college is as stuffy any more as most were when I was an undergraduate, but the okay groves of Academe have remained relatively sober, and it was a pleasure to see a place where the spontaneous and even the calculating zany is not only tolerated but encouraged.

"There is no possibility here of an administration separate from faculty and students. It's just the opposite. It's possible for the students to tyrannize the place."

EDWARD APGAR, PROFESSOR OF PHYSICS

On my first foray, I made the drive up to southern Vermont from New York flushed with the ribald encouragement of my friends and colleagues, all of whom assumed that I was bound for some fleshly Xanadu, some bohemian synthesis of Denmark and Tahiti, where the women would be blond, bare-breasted, brilliant, and excessively friendly to travelers.

As I crossed the Vermont border there was nothing in view to reinforce this garish pipe dream. White-fenced fields marched away from the shoulder of the road, advancing politely on cozy white clapboard farmhouses with red barns and red cows. It was all Grandma Moses Vermont, lovely and prim and perfectly circumscribed by a New England farmer's respect for order and neatness. Over a rise I came abruptly upon Old Bennington, a beautiful, largely unspoiled New England town, the white spire of First Church and the grey stone shaft of the Revolutionary War battle monument vying for dominance over a dialogue of great white Colonial houses, in any one of which Claudette Colbert could quite feasibly have spent the war, awaiting Walter Pidgeon's return. After negotiating an additional five miles downhill through the urban detritus of Bennington proper, full of EAT signs and discount gas stations, I came on the gates of Bennington College, and a road leading up a green hill, cool and sylvan. On the crest of that hill stood the college, though you could not have proved it by me at the time.

I kept driving around past red barns and chicken houses, thinking it had to be around here *somewhere,* and there it was all the time, looking most astonishingly like a lot of red barns and chicken houses. There were, on exploration, some rather more imposing structures: a vague sort of Mount Vernon, in brick with white galleries, which I later learned was the Commons, an enormous U-shaped red horse barn, used for administration, a modern library, and twelve spacious white frame Colonial houses, dead ringers for the Old Bennington houses I had lately seen. These, it emerged, were the dormitories, and it seemed to me then that no girl, however wealthy, could do other than improve her living conditions by moving into one of them. They and the Commons form three sides of a wide, sloping green. On the fourth side, beyond a fieldstone fence, the hill drops abruptly away, providing the college center with a panoramic view of the valley and mountains beyond. It is a gentle, stunning site. But none of it had anything to do with the place I'd come to see, which I knew to be a hotbed of liberal education where 350 girls did exactly as they pleased for four years, without grades or examinations, mostly dancing and painting like crazy. I later learned that Frank Lloyd Wright had been equally disconcerted on his first visit to Bennington. Grumpily he surveyed all the Vermont farm charm of this avant garde institution. His sour evaluation: "The place is a living lie."

In fact, the traditional restraint of the college architecture is more attributable to the founders' lack of money than to any conservative residue in their taste, though that was certainly an element. For the college was first conceived as a source for the rejuvenation of Old Bennington, where it was thought that many of the gracious old homes could be acquired to house a college. It was all the dream of the minister of First Church, Dr. Arthur Ravi Booth, in 1923, and what he wanted more than anything else was to fill up his church on Sundays. As had happened in communities all over New England, the coming of the railroads had pulled the vitality of the village off the hilltop and down onto the flatland, and by the 1920's the old heart of the village sat cool, white, and anachronistic on its hill, underpopulated and dying save for the summer influx of vacationing cityfolk. It was to these wealthy and well-connected people that Dr. Ravi Booth applied, and it was a matter of happy chance that most of them were dedicated to the idea that if they were to do anything for education, it ought to be something in aid of modern educational thinking.

The time was uniquely right. Conventional women's colleges in the Northeast were many and crowded. New prep schools, practicing the progressive ideas of John Dewey, had nowhere to send their students. And everywhere in the country, a lot of quick-made money was looking for a home. In the early 1920's, anything seemed possible. Prominent progressive educators and other influential people rallied to the campaign for a new sort of college for women, a free and experimental environment, a place for risks in curriculum and in organization.

The founders were in sight of their goal when there came the crash of 1929. Suddenly the money was gone, and by 1930, stockbrokers were jumping from windows instead of making good their pledges to Bennington. Even the pledge of land in Old Bennington was withdrawn. But then a farm in North Bennington was offered, and the founders adjusted their budget to a fraction of first estimates, and the college limped into functioning existence in the fall of 1932. If it looks a little like Old Bennington from the outside, it's a small enough concession to the people who worked during

overwhelmingly difficult times to bring the college to any
sort of life at all. And after all, the girls at the college have
never done much to fill up old First Church.

The principal aim of the founders was that the college
should be "so administered that in the remote future the
best thought of the day, not the dead hand of tradition, will
rule." In thirty-five years the college has struggled to keep
faith with that admonition. The curious thing is that the
rest of American education has been catching up with Bennington ever since, and it is far from the outlandish place
it once was. There is an uneasiness among some faculty and
students that the experimental nature of the college is being
bled out. Thirty-five years ago it was so much easier to be
avant garde.

*"In art, we are the most avant garde institution in the U.S.
We pick out the latest, the hottest."*

PAUL FEELEY, PAINTER

*"Social protest is unlikely here. Most people are upper class,
with no experience of social injustice. These things don't happen
to them in any immediate sense. Speakers come here, tell us
horrifying things—but the girls don't pay attention if they
don't* speak *well."*

A STUDENT

What greatly scandalized most conventional observers in
the early years was that Bennington had so few rules. No
required courses of study. No competitive marks. No curfew
for the girls. The emphasis outside was always on "no" this
and "no" that, rarely on the positive innovations of the Bennington program, the most salutary effect of which is to in-

volve the student utterly in her own education, as the chief participant and director, a role which most students elsewhere never play. It is a lonely and rigorous role for a girl of eighteen, and not every girl can or wishes to play it. Attrition at Bennington is very nearly 50 percent. For those who respond, however, it can be a maturing and highly joyous experience.

A Bennington freshman begins with four courses, selected with the advice of her faculty counselor. Protocol requires that she apply to each teacher personally for admission to his course. The system requires that she meet with her counselor for at least one hour each week. Practically, the interaction is usually much more frequent. The student is advised of her individual progress by means of midterm and end-of-term written reports from each of her teachers, frankly evaluating her strengths and weaknesses. There are no "marks." As one teacher said, "A girl is never 'finished.' She never knows exactly where she stands." After the eleven-week fall term comes a nine-week winter nonresident term, during which the student is supposed to get a job, preferably a paying job, hopefully in the area of her major interest. Her employer writes a report of her performance, and she of her experience, and these are added to a voluminous file of reports which includes the minutes of faculty meetings regularly held to discuss her progress. The student spends the eleven-week spring term back on campus, and the files grow thicker. And so it goes for four years, all of it spent under the closest sort of scrutiny, until each girl's career could literally be measured in inches and feet of engorged file folders.

This remorseless searchlight on a girl's progress can make

for a lonely life, and there are no conventional crutches. As William Fels, late and much-beloved president of Bennington, once said, "If a college is to be mature, it must eschew sentimentality and childishness." Out go alma maters, candlelight services, pennants and stickers, the degrading of freshmen, baton twirlers, cheerleaders, stadiums, any athletics that are not truly amateur—and with them the paid coaches, fraternities and sororities and their rituals, proms and queens. (In fact, Bennington did once have a queen. In late 1964, one Alice Ruby was named National Collegiate Scholastic Queen by an IBM computer. Though it was not a beauty contest, Alice *was* photogenic and hygienic, got to wear a tiara and pose with Charlton Heston in chain mail. But as the college bulletin admitted, Bennington scarcely knew "what to do" with Queen Alice.)

"A long procession of Bennington College girls, appropriately costumed for the celebration of Dante's 700th birthday Wednesday evening, wades through ankle deep grass from the fiery depths of Hell (the college dump) to Purgatory, on the commons lawn. Claude Fredericks, literature teacher, who is playing the role of Virgil, helps a student across a Vermont stone wall . . . The girls were served fried chicken and potato salad for dinner in Purgatory, then went on to Paradise, in the Jennings garden, for dessert."

CAPTION FROM THE *Bennington Banner*, MAY 27, 1965

In the absence of academic competition, a girl works only against herself. She lives in a similar isolation, with few organized activities. There are few rules—only those the students themselves make. There are no housemothers to hear alibis, and no alibis are necessary. There is no hiding place.

It is a ruthless education in personal responsibility and it works a burden on the girl and on everyone she encounters. Simple dating, for example, is not so simple at Bennington. "It's awkward," a junior told me. "A boy comes up here knowing you don't *have* to be back at any special time. There is no witching hour. It's a challenge to his masculinity that he may not want to face. And it gives the girl no ready 'out.' She can't say she has to get back."

As Fels once told entering students: "Bennington is a difficult place for new students. This is because it is not school, but life . . . all choices are up to you. . . . You have, as Margaret Mead has suggested, a four-year moratorium from the irreparable. . . . You have an unexampled opportunity to form an identity and a life on the sound grounds of knowledge and experience. We will cherish and nourish you in this most personal of pilgrimages, but like Pilgrim himself, the progress must be yours."

The girls accept this challenge with ferocity. For the girl who worries about not having an excuse to leave her date will just as conscientiously state her destination if she decides instead to spend the night with him. This issue came up recently because of a blunder by a new member of the administration. The community rule provides that a girl may sign out of her dorm to anywhere she pleases, and stay the night, so long as she is where she says she will be. And if that is to be at the Bide-a-Wee Motel with a Williams senior, that is what she puts down in the sign-out book. The new member of the administration stopped by at a dorm sign-out book one night and saw, to her horror, that a girl had indeed signed out to the Bide-a-Wee. Outraged, she called the girl at the motel and condemned her for a harlot.

The college reacted swiftly. The girls called a community meeting at which they demanded to know if the administration expected them to lie about their whereabouts in the sign-out book. The vote (administration, faculty, and students all vote) massively favored personal integrity, the interference with the girl's personal social life was condemned, and the new member of the administration got an embarrassing lesson in real democracy.

Says Fels' successor in the presidency, Dr. Edward J. Blaustein: "This is a remarkable place. It shouldn't *be*, and it is. It's a kind of implementation, an embodiment, of profound philosophical stuff like the Value of Freedom, and like Freedom Breeds Responsibility, and like the proposition that theory and practice complement each other in many ways. Bennington shows us democracy as a vigorous and rigorous exercise. I would go so far as to say that not another college in America is as democratic."

"This is a pay-as-you-go outfit, and if you want to go here, you pay dough."

PAUL FEELEY

Nor is another college in America so expensive. It costs $3,450 a year to attend Bennington, for the simple reason that education of this intensity, on such a small numerical basis (a student-faculty ratio of seven to one) is the most expensive education to come by. And Bennington has only a tiny endowment of about $1,800,000. Some financial aid can be given to about 30 percent of the students. But as one teacher said, "A person with an income of five thousand dollars would never be able to send a daughter to Bennington, and that saddens me. I wish some angel would come along and endow some scholarships." Blaustein's plan is to broaden the base—to enlarge the enrollment slightly and to build new facilities. His fund-raising campaign, Bennington's first, aims to raise $17,000,000, pleading the college's cause as an institution of "national dimension." He is building new dormitories, a new science building, a new art building and art gallery, and a new center for the performing arts. When Blaustein is done, it will no longer be possible to mistake Bennington for a Vermont farm. But he does not intend that any new building should have what he calls "monument quality." "I am not for personal expression in architecture," he says. "I myself tend to think that you should not ask creative people to work in somebody's personal expression."

Blaustein has a faculty full of creative people, the only kind Bennington wants. Academic degrees are unimportant. Says a college publication: "Bennington recognizes no academic rank or hierarchy, does not regard a Ph.D. as a requirement for teaching, and allows that excellence in teaching might consist simply in teaching very well. . . ." Nor has the college any interest in the "publish or perish" pattern that prevails in most American colleges. Faculty members are all busy with their own work. They are creative. They produce. And students benefit richly. "A lot of our staffing," says Blaustein, "results from the fact that non-organization men are in flight from structure elsewhere. From the beginning, Bennington couldn't afford to pay high salaries, so we got good young men, with a built-in turnover. It's one of the ways to maintain excitement in an institution. Creativity is self-reinforcing."

Among those who now teach or have taught at Bennington are some of the most pivotal artists and scholars in every field of contemporary American culture. To name a few: Lawrence Alloway, W. H. Auden, Kenneth Burke, Francis Fergusson, Wallace Fowlie, Erich Fromm, Nathan Glazer, Francis Golffing, Stanley Edgar Hyman, Bernard Malamud, Howard Nemerov, Richard Neutra, Theodore Roethke, Allan Seagar, Jules Olitski, Paul Feeley, Anthony Caro. Demonstrably, Bennington is a good place for people who want to get on with their own work.

The girls are terrifyingly bright, for the college's admissions policies are frighteningly selective, and all those eager, questing minds are a stimulus to a teacher's own work. But the girls are a trial, too, because of the methods Bennington brags about, and the personal demands on the teacher far outstrip anything he will have encountered in the cooler atmosphere of most other colleges. Each girl is encouraged by the system to think she is what grade school teachers used to call, scornfully, "the only pebble on the beach." This anxious self-absorption has unfortunate social ramifications. The girls rush up to teachers wherever they find them, indifferent to what a man may be doing at the time, breaking into conversations, thrusting themselves forward. On a campus walk with Howard Nemerov one morning, I counted three girls in the space of a city block who bellied up to us, breaking in to say, "Hey! Listen!" and then to go on to Nemerov about personal scholastic matters. There was never any apology for interrupting, nor even any sense of awareness that they *had* interrupted. A teacher usually bears this with patience and kindness. But unless he is interested in a temporary illicit affair with a student, or is available for marriage, he must take pains not to be on call twenty-four hours a day. He usually makes it clear to his students, and especially to his advisees, that he does not expect to be telephoned or called upon at home without prior arrangement. "You've got to have somewhere to hide," one teacher told me. "Otherwise they'd eat you alive."

Many of the girls carry this MeMeMe fixation back with them into the workaday world, where it sits even less well. I know one bright, intense girl who, in her first job after Bennington, rapidly grew disgusted with the business procedures in her New York office. Within a few weeks, having had all she could take, she charged into the office of her mild-mannered boss and "set him straight" in the best Bennington style, sparing him none of her sharply articulated indignation. And he fired her. Suddenly she was a bright, intense Bennington graduate out of work, and she wasn't the first of her kind to come a cropper this way. "We are not teaching what sells," says Blaustein. "There's time enough for that later." Unhappily, what often sells is good manners, and this is a painful way to have to learn them.

In its own circle of Eastern colleges, Bennington has a distinct reputation for pushy girls. Not just bohemian girls, free spirits, but pushy, bad-mannered girls. And it hampers their recruiting efforts. Said one freshman, "None of my friends came here and none of them wanted me to come. They felt it was too far out, in the worst sense of being far out. They thought the girls were rude—and really too many of them are. And they thought there wasn't a serious central core of intellectuality, but that's just not so."

Another freshman I talked to was a core of intellectuality all to herself. Radcliffe had offered her "advanced placement" because of her promise, and for already having studied calculus, physics, honors English, French, history—and Chinese, at which she was quite proficient. But she took Bennington instead—Bennington, which "doesn't bother with advanced placement; they don't have to make the point." Her own remarks explain the Bennington experience so well that I'll let her speak for herself: "If I had drawn a plan for my ideal college, Bennington would be it—except that I'd have placed it closer to a large city, and closer to men. I really need to meet men's minds.

"The faculty are all professionals, and they let you watch them. My counselor is a fantastic historian. He pretends to be a cynic, but really, he's not. He's one of the most astute men I've ever met. I spend at least an hour a week with him. It's a very saving thing. I look forward to it. I need it. I need to be with somebody who makes sense and is not a girl.

"He has seven others, just like me.

"This is one of the few places where the emphasis in the program is on learning a discipline instead of groping, learning facts that just may apply. It is the doing that I think is the whole key to this thing called a liberal education. For example, I'm in the baby music class, and I've already composed a trio for violin, viola, and cello. It's been played by competent musicians in a workshop and it sounded fine. I do think, though, in the music department, that in their search for the new they tend to play too little of the old.

"I am not a so-called typical B student; and I'm not a dancer and not an artist. But I may very well be any of those things before I leave. I know if I'd gone to Radcliffe or Bryn Mawr, I would have been stuck in the social sciences. Verbal people tend to stick together. Here I have the idea that the door is still open."

In all the girl said, somehow the most touching item was her expression of a need for male company, an attitude she does not harbor alone. Yet the question of coeducation for Bennington is raised every year at community meetings and every year the proposition is soundly voted down by the students. Most of the girls are possessive about their academic advantages, some of them even paranoid. "When we invite our dates to class," said one girl defensively, "the teachers are more sharp. I think that's very insulting." Beyond jealousy, there is also the suspicion that Bennington methods would not attract Prince Charming. "Men at Bennington!" another girl barked. "What kind of creeps would we get?"

In fact, Bennington has been just barely coed for a long time. Every year, six or seven full fellowships are given to men, after competitions, by the dance and drama departments, which need men for their productions. For the boys it's a full-time job of rehearsal and performance, but they also have the opportunity to obtain a valuable, if unusual, academic degree, and they are constantly involved with the sort of work they plan to do professionally later. Alan Arkin, for example, went to Bennington. None of the boys now there would mind following in Arkin's famous footsteps. Nor is it disagreeable for a young man to be surrounded by 350 intense young ladies. "They think of us as the ravening horde," one boy told me. "We're very, you know, suspect. But that's not a bad image, if you think about it."

Feminine society, even at Bennington, does have its convent aspects, and as a lone male visitor, I often stumbled, unaware, into trouble. Once, visiting the pottery barn, I heard a great hue and cry from the sculpture studio just down the hill. The pottery instructor and I thought nothing of it until a messenger came along from the studio, requesting that I leave the neighborhood. It seems that there was a life-study class going on, with a nude model, and the girls were afraid I might peek in at her through the windows. In fact, the afternoon sun had cast such a glare on the studio windows that no one could have seen in from outside, and if the class had kept their mouths shut, I would never have been the wiser. Instead, I departed to a chorus of girlish titters, as if from a scandalized harem. On another occasion, over dinner in town with a few girls, the conversation touched briefly on sex. Late that night, one of the girls called my hotel. She was distressed, she said, that our conversation had taken that turn, and she asked me to meet her next day on campus. When I did, I arrived to face a sort of star chamber of hostile and suspicious faces. Inasmuch as I had raised the issue of sex, did I then intend to write "that sort of article"? What *were* my intentions, exactly? I felt like the culprit at a shotgun wedding.

But for all their infrequent attempts at Victorian manners, the girls at Bennington, by reason of their dedication to learning by doing, have perhaps more than their share of sexual and psychiatric disasters, though not a great deal more trouble in these delicious but dangerous byways than do most college students today. When I went to see Dr. Dorothy Hager, the college physician, she gave me a straight draught of common sense and practical thinking. "We probably do have a higher percentage of students with problems than most colleges," she said, "but we keep better track of them than most. We don't have a psychiatrist on the faculty now. When I came here in 1941, we did, and when he left we had no less than Erich Fromm, who was available on Mondays. Now we have Mrs. Florey, a psychiatric social worker. She sees about a hundred girls a year." Mindful of the free-and-easy sign-out arrangements, I asked about pregnancies. "Oh, maybe ten girls a semester *fear* they're pregnant," she said. "But it's usually no more than three. We take the usual line—we cannot suggest an abortionist— but there is somebody in every house who knows where to go. Mostly I see the girls afterward to check. There was the case of a girl who went to Mexico—she had a bad infection. I have to wonder if she will ever have another child. I don't tell the Barn [the Barn is the Bennington word for the administration] when this kind of thing comes up. I don't even write these things down." When I left Dr. Hager I understood why one student had said of her, in a rare encomium, "Yeah, do talk to Hager. She's a pretty cool old bag."

She is also an eminently available old bag, for the infirmary is in the Commons building, just off the main lounge and life center of the college. In Commons the girls pick up their mail, eat ("SHOES MUST BE WORN IN THE DINING-ROOM"), and recreate. A snack bar operates in the corridor when the dining room is shut, and in the same corridor, student "galleys" are posted. These are broadsides written by students on any subject under the sun, and obligingly mimeographed and displayed by the college. The girls customarily take a long look at the corridor bulletin boards before entering the lounge, a large, tile-floored room with a fireplace at one end. Here, plastic cushions deck the metal furniture, and coffee and soft drinks ooze from paper containers into puddles on the formica tables. There are large windows gazing out onto the green, the window seats often occupied by lounging louts, looking for dates and self-consciously preening in wheat jeans and sandals. (You do *not* come courting to Bennington in a three-button suit.) The dress is decidedly outdoorsy for winter and summer, with bare feet preferred in any season. Many boys are afraid to try their luck at Bennington, and those who have the guts often lack the cool to carry it off. "The animals," said one girl. "They hang around, leering and grabbing, and you're supposed to *love* it."

It is in and out of this aggressively bohemian atmosphere, this shambles of a daily meeting place, that the exciting intellectual life of Bennington passes. "One day in Commons," a male student told me, "I noticed a big stack of two-by-fours in the corner. It stayed there for weeks and weeks, and I figured the workers must be on strike. My friends are always kidding me about having no eye for art, and I really don't dig this structural sculpture stuff of Caro's, I mean, stuff is always looming at you on the lawn and all, and I decided to have some fun with this stack of lumber. I came in one day and I said, Ooooh and Aaaah over this lumber, I said My God, what balance, what imagination, you know, like I was appreciating it as a work of art. And do you know, it turned out it *was* a work of art. Stacked lumber, my God, I thought it was a joke and everybody praised me for finally seeing the artistic values."

On the third floor of the Commons is the main auditorium of the college. The dance department gives its workshop programs there, drawing an enormous crowd for the little

town of Bennington. It's a friendly, almost folksy scene—
when it's time for the curtain, the audience breaks away from
its Cokes and coffee downstairs and climbs the two flights into
the auditorium. It's a motley crowd—townspeople looking
rather dressed up and square, faculty and their wives looking like faculty and wives anywhere, the husband featuring
tweeds and leather-patched elbows, the wife tending toward
small prints in her dress, her hair in a bun and knitting on
her knee, a child or two, pigtails and tights. There are always
friendly old dogs, campus dogs, smelly but placid, wandering
up and down the aisles and glancing occasionally at the
stage. Every dance piece performed is choreographed by a
dance major, and every piece gets at least three curtain calls.
Mostly the pieces have to do with a lonely girl who can't
get or hold men—there is a lot of running around the stage
(searching but not finding) and then there is some leaning
toward one another (ecstatic encounter) and an awful lot of
miserable flopping and sinking into the floor (he left).
There is very little humor in these dance programs, but they
are very prettily danced, and rather appealingly sad.

Just behind the Commons, in one wing of the Barn, is
Paul Grey's theater. Paul Grey is a newcomer to Bennington's drama department, and Bennington likes him so much
it has built him his own experimental theater, in the round.
Grey likes experiment. "I'm either twenty-five years ahead
or behind," he says, "depending on who I'm talking to."
Grey has taught elsewhere but most of his experience is in
the commercial ("not always so commercial") theater as an
actor and director. Grey wears his hair to his shoulders if he
feels like it, and he indulges in a colorful vocabulary. That
sort of thing sits uneasily on most campuses but, as Grey

puts it, "Bennington is one of the last refuges for outlaws." Bennington's acceptance of Grey has bothered him. "Most people don't like me," he insists. "I'm a walking alienation effect. I'm not social. I don't drink. I'm terrible at cocktail parties." And finally, "I don't make friends."

But Bennington persists in liking him, try as he will to have it otherwise. His first effort for the college was a production of Jean Genet's *The Balcony,* in which all the ripe young ladies were cast as prostitutes. It was a great success, even with the mothers who journeyed up to see it, though Grey had the girls reading pornography for weeks to get a sense of their roles. Grey aims to do "extreme work in original areas." "Somebody said to me," he recalled, " 'You prepare students for a theater that doesn't exist.' You bet your sweet ass I do." Grey doesn't think he'll last. "Somebody always comes along and says, 'Okay, show me something in profits, wise guy.' " But at Bennington he doesn't have to worry. One of his freshman students put it this way. "In the history of the theater," she said, "we're not doing anything revolutionary, but college-theaterwise, we are."

At an intermission during one of Grey's productions, I heard a Bennington girl saying to her date, "My roommate makes glass sculptures. Every night she's in our room smashing milk bottles and mirrors. Wham—glass everywhere. I wish some morning she'd get up and forget her slippers!" Real art and real scholarship are never placid, never uneventful. They are marked with cries of pain and pleasure, messy with the prickly shards that creativity leaves behind. And so I found myself siding with the girl who breaks the glass. That is, after all, how glass gets broken. As a freshman once said to me, "Bennington is a question of possibilities, so many possibilities, and it can induce intoxication or terror. Here, you have got to be seriously directed or strongly motivated. For people like this, Bennington is almost Utopia."

atlantic city: a fugue for foghorns

some years ago, a good-looking, rather glamorous New York lady writer signed a network contract to write a documentary series for radio. The producer, gathering up the papers, remarked casually that everything was dandy and that he would pick the lady up at her apartment on Saturday morning at ten, for a trip to Atlantic City.

"I beg your pardon," she said icily, tugging at her beige toque. "Are we writing the show in Atlantic City?"

"No, honey," he said. "You and I are spending the weekend in Atlantic City."

Moving smoothly to the desk, the lady writer snatched up the contract and, in a manner she hoped Rosalind Russell would be proud of, she ripped it dramatically down the middle. "Let me ask you something," she demanded of the producer. "Do I really *look* like Atlantic City to you? You might at least have said Cannes."

The fact is that for many decades "The World's Playground," as the city styles itself, has been the major home for weekend affairs exported from New York and Philadelphia. With its thousands of hotel bedrooms and acres of beach and dark, underpopulated bars, Atlantic City offers the most accessible anonymity at its end of the Eastern Seaboard. Owing to a nice discretion, appropriate to a city of innkeepers, this aspect of Atlantic City is the sole attraction which the city fathers have never advertised. But the glamorous lady writer knew about it well enough not to want to be in on it.

Many others have found it exactly to their taste, not by any means only those bent on extracurricular mischief. Atlantic City is a great place to go if you want to get some work done. Edna Ferber wrote *The Ice Palace* there, holed up in a big, beach-front hotel. Thornton Wilder used to retreat there to write plays. Just about every big annual professional convention has wound up there more than once— and anyone who has been to one can tell you that conventions are not so much for fun as for job-oriented back-slapping and commercial hustle. So if you are ever on a toot with a lady not your wife, or if you write, or if you just belong to something or other—or even if you just like sandy beaches and crowds by the millions—you will find yourself in Atlantic City sooner or later. This is a marvelous thing for the city's economy but it does suggest that the World's Playground is, as in the thinking of the lady writer, a trifle ordinary. I can see the point but, in a broader sense, I can't agree with it, because I was there this winter with the family and we thought it was very special.

I have always had a thing about seaside resorts out of season. There is a lonely, haunted quality about them that I find poignant and intriguing. I remember a winter weekend at Knokke, a Channel resort on the Belgian coast, when it never stopped raining and we sat on glassed-in terraces and watched the rain trickling down the panes, distorting our view of the wet boardwalk beyond. We felt like characters in *Separate Tables* and were very melancholy and very happy. My wife and I hoped for something like that when we set off for Atlantic City, though we knew it would be different from that because we were taking the children, Dorothy and Kate, five and three. Actually, *I* took the children, and drove down from New York on a Thursday afternoon. Jean was to join us the next day.

Naturally, it rained all the way down, and this pleased me and got my hopes up. The children became very excited as we crossed the causeway to the sandbar on which the city sits, and we could see all the towering hotels and bright lights and smell the sea. We headed for the Chalfonte-Haddon Hall, which is actually two hotels run as one and has literally thousands of rooms and a complex of lobbies and ballrooms that could be measured in hectares. There was an awful lot of flash about arriving under the marquee and being advanced upon by liveried servants brandishing glistening black umbrellas; and to be ushered with murmured courtesies and exclamations of delight through such mammoth public rooms was as stunning an experience for me as it clearly was for the gaping children. None of us could bring himself to speak above a whisper for hours afterward.

Installed in our rooms, rising to the occasion against an unreasonable panic, Dorothy, Kate, and I proceeded in an orderly fashion to the Wedgwood Room, where Dinner was Being Served. The ambiance was perfect—there were hundreds of tables covered in white damask; vast chandeliers tinkled overhead; there were perhaps fifteen people dining in the huge room. The sounds were few and quite subdued—the crystal tinkle, the tap of knife on china plate, the wind-blown rain rushing at the windows, and underneath it all, the piped strains of "I'm Always True to You, Darlin', in My Fashion," in a sort of 1949 arrangement with lots of sax. It was the most delightful dinner out in my memory, with the most charming companions. We were a quiet but animated trio; despite our somewhat forced good manners, quite the liveliest table in the Wedgwood Room that night.

The ladies were very popular with the waitresses, who lavished a lot of attention on them and were probably glad of the distraction. The waitresses talked to me about how Kate looked like me and how Dorothy probably looked like her mother and how people ought to raise their children. After my coffee was brought, they invited the ladies to inspect the kitchens, which Dorothy and Kate thought were thrilling and exotic. Since there were so many more cooks than customers, all the good times were being had on the far side of the pantry. While I waited at the table (rather sad because I had not been asked to see the kitchens), I thought how far we have come toward the egalitarian society, and how far the Russians reportedly still have to go. The Wedgwood Room was a sort of utopian society under the chandeliers of a vanished aristocracy, and though I was playing the role of Capitalist for the occasion, and the waitresses were playing Workers, we were really all in it together and very damned matey at that.

After dinner, we gawked along the shopping arcades until the rain stopped, and then went out to walk along the boardwalk and to peek into a couple of the neighboring hotels. The ladies were absolutely spooked by the vast, elaborate, empty public rooms we tiptoed through. I remember one cathedrallike solarium, full of stately palms and stern, forbidding furniture, with a gurgling fountain at one end. There was a greenish cast to the light and a ghostly glow through the wet windows and not a soul in the place but us. Kate said, "Daddy, is there somebody *in* here?" Dorothy's reaction was the same every time I ventured into a new rococo cavern. "No, Daddy," she would say, pulling on my hand, "it's not allowed."

We stayed out scandalously late, wandering the boardwalk in complete solitude, and on the way back passed the wax museum. There was a wax lady in the window, reclining on a chaise and "breathing" rather ostentatiously, and the children liked her. But there was another wax lady visible at the ticket booth inside. She was not breathing but she looked shockingly real and right away the children said, "Let's go." So we bedded down without further incident, and slept to the sound of the sea.

Friday morning was damp and foggy, but after breakfast we walked out across the boardwalk onto the beach, past the spindly drift fences and empty sunning chairs, right down to the water. Dorothy and Kate raced to the water's edge, halfway over a laid deck, the final half over deep sand. The surf was up, the waves came crashing and rolling out of the fog, and we played together that irresistible game of tag with the waves, running toward the incoming tide, then fleeing from the water as it pursued us back up the beach. The sand was wet, rain-pelted, and pocked with the tracks of horses that had come that way, and we scampered around and fell down in the sticky sand and made a mess of ourselves.

The fog was so dense that we couldn't see the hotels or the boardwalk, and we might have been on a deserted beach except for the looming shapes of the piers that extended on dark pilings far out into the fog. On the far side of a nearby jetty, a thousand sea gulls were taking their ease, wading in the water. Kate giggled as she watched the waves wash over their tiny feet and set them adrift. Dorothy preferred to creep up on the tightly packed, cawing conventions of birds, then run among them suddenly to set up a screaming flap, sending hundreds of gulls into flight above her head.

At the foot of a stunted pier we were surprised to come upon a solitary bather, sitting on the sand wearing only a black wool bathing suit. He was reading the *Newark News* and digging his toes into the sand and was apparently under the impression that it was July. He seemed to be basking in the chilly, foggy air, perfectly oblivious of us. We marched on, marveling, to a pony ring, to converse with the ponies, and then we climbed back up on the boardwalk and tried to get the sticky sand off our feet by stamping our sneakers vigorously. It didn't do any good—especially not for Kate, who hasn't really mastered stamping yet—but it *felt* like the right thing to do.

We strolled along the boardwalk again, stopping here and

there at the storefront auction houses to see what was happening. At every shop a handful of dubious strollers had been sucked inside by the hypnotic spiel of an auctioneer. The spielers are master performers. With their patter routines, punctuated by the thump of a fist on the podium, they rustle up more entertainment for nothing than you can buy on Broadway at $9.50 a seat. There is the additional titillation, of course, that you *may* find yourself spending money against your better judgment. Says the cat to the mouse: "Risk a quarter with me, ladies and gentlemen, only one quarter, and not only do you get a prize, which is in this box and which I do not yet tell you the contents thereof, though it is guaranteed to be worth hard cash well in excess of one single quarter, hard cash, ladies and gentlemen, but you also, simultaneously and at the very same time, buy a chance on this marvelous shaggy dog which I hold here in my hand—can you see it, lady?— a dog that does not bite. And I want to tell you, friends, I'd like to be a dog myself. A dog's life in this day and time beats the twenty-five-cent existence of a boardwalk auctioneer, yes sir or madam. Now who has a quarter? *This* lady has a quarter. I know this lady has a quarter. No? Madam, where are you from? Philadelphia, the lady says Philadelphia. Now I wish you'd tell me something, and all these good people here: How can you look so nice and be so stingy?"

Dorothy pulled my sleeve. "Daddy," she said, "what does that man want us to win?"

We strolled on past candy stores and toy stores and special discount stores. One outfit had more jewelry and gewgaws in its window than can ever before have been gathered together in one small space—and a sign in the window insisted that Everything Must Go This Week. For that to happen, the storekeeper must have been praying for either one million customers or one real fool.

Finally we got down as far as the Planters Peanuts establishment, and stood outside to admire the monocled, mechanized, man-sized Mr. Peanut, who spins around endlessly and jauntily on the roof of the marquee. Kate persisted in calling him Mrs. Peanutbuttermaker, which was okay by me but might well alarm the image-conscious folks at Planters.

After Jean arrived, our weekend began in earnest. We launched ourselves into a rolling chair, all four of us, for a long, whirring ride up and down the boardwalk, huddled snugly under a mammoth lap robe. We spent a cold afternoon in the sultry confines of the hotel's heated pool, splashing around at the shallow end while Dorothy and Kate insisted they could swim and in the next breath shrieked, "Don't let go, Daddy!" On Saturday morning, while Jean was treating herself to a massage by a lady who once pressed and pummeled Lady Bird, I took a long architectural tour of the hotels, which viewed in a row seem like a flotilla of Jules Verne luxury ocean liners, inexplicably beached on the sandbar. No two are alike but, if any architectural theme might be said to dominate, I would have to call it a sort of Abyssinian Byzantine. For pure fantasia, and hang the cost, the Walt Disney medal should certainly go to the Marlborough-Blenheim, which runs the gamut of styles from Early Egyptian Massive to Maine Cottage Bulbous. I believe there is nothing quite like it in the world, which many may think is a good thing. But I love it, and cherish the delight I felt at being lost in it for an hour. In one of its huge, chair-lined, sun-filled corridors, I saw a frighteningly antique lady edge forward toward the limited visual field of a gentleman so elderly and diminished that his slumped figure scarcely emerged from the cushions. "Not much sun today," she shouted at him by way of openers. "Eh?" he inquired, amiably. "The sun isn't shining," she shrieked. "No," he said, "not much sun today." This established, the lady edged on, smiling.

I know two couples who honeymooned at the Marlborough-Blenheim, and they loved it, but now I understand why, when I asked one guy who else usually stayed there, he replied, "Mostly very, very old ladies . . . and their mothers." Next time we go to Atlantic City, that's where I'm checking in.

On past the M-B, I came to the Convention Hall, and persuaded a guard to let me peek in. Not only did I want to see the hallowed place in which Hubert H. Humphrey was nominated for the vice-presidency, but I was also eager to see a place not in Texas where indoor football is regularly played. Convention Hall is the real economic core of Atlantic City, and it has proved to be tall enough for LBJ, deep enough for Miss America, and wide enough for Bert Parks' bleacher-to-bleacher smile. As I brooded over the vast area, I fancied I heard music. It was the music of my country, and Bert Parks was singing it: "Theeere she goees, Miss America, mahee ideeeeeeeel."

Before we left Atlantic City on Sunday afternoon, there was a last pilgrimage I had to make. For years I have been a dedicated Monopoly fan, and it was important to me to visit some of those pink, purple and blue-grey properties I have so often lost to my cackling friends. For it is Atlantic City that Monopoly is all about, from four-hundred-dollar Boardwalk to sixty-dollar Baltic Avenue. The streets I could find all seemed to work out as on the Monopoly board, right down to poor old Baltic. The next time you are stuck with that property, you might find it diverting to consider what you've actually got. There aren't many houses, and none of them green, but there are the Ratner Pest Control, the police garage, and the Atlantic City Sewerage Co. And there is a hotel, the Liberty Hotel, which accommodates transients by day or week. I was glad to see that the Liberty Hotel is red; it's good to know that some things in life are real.

esalen: coming to my senses

   i got in touch with my body this winter—I made contact with my Self—and it was the best trip I've ever had. I would like to stay on that trip for the rest of my life, but I'm full of doubts, now that I'm away from people who feel what I mean. It is rather scary in here, by Myself, with no one to help me and family and friends listening to me with widening disbelief and, sometimes, alarm. I don't blame them; I can hear myself arguing passionately, with an evangelical fervor, that it is possible to be aware, to be happy, to know the unlimited joy that we are unquestionably equipped for; that it is not necessary to be an intellect attached to an insensate body; that most of us are really not alive at all. Funny, isn't it, that you argue for the possibility of joy, and people know instantly that you are some kind of a nut.

I had heard quite a lot about the Esalen Institute, at Big Sur on the California coast and in San Francisco, where it has a relationship more or less tenuous, depending on who is talking, with Grace Cathedral and the Episcopal Diocese of California. This ostensible connection with Episcopalians reassured me, because the activities of Esalen seem wildly experimental and bizarre to the well-trained tweed, while Episcopalianism is somehow still safely associated, for the same tweed, with convention, money, Peck & Peck, and a spare but aesthetic ritual in terribly good taste. Godly, of course, but not enough to bother anybody.

With that lozenge of assurance deeply filed in my Cough Center, expecting to participate in sensitivity sandwiches (as shown on the CBS Sunday News) and communal bathing (not shown on CBS), confident of my detachment from any—God forbid—involvement, I set off for San Francisco, the city which, of all in the world, I love most. Stumbling off the plane, drugged nearly insensible on transcontinental Technicolor and portable brandy, I sniffed just a little Bay Area air en route to rent a car. The car was itself reassuring: big, fat, and fast-back, and very assertively yellow—the perfect tool for aging sports.

Smoothly my yellow car shot me down the peninsula past San Jose. Within an hour and a half I was negotiating the cross-country route to Highway One, directly among the busy firing ranges of Fort Ord. I passed swiftly through Monterey, a town that looks as if it had all been dropped out of an airplane, and Carmel, which appears to have been constructed entirely by the Seven Dwarfs, coming finally into the Big Sur coastal country, which starts, for me, when the last thatched roof is behind and the scenery takes over. The Monterey radio had, meanwhile, lots to sell me: "Men! Don't divorce your wife if she won't clean house. Hire Lafayette Housecleaning Service and keep your wife as a pet!" Or, "Men! Keep a Sante Fe cigar in your face and your wife in her place!"

Coming out of Carmel, I found myself confronting the Pacific Ocean head on. I turned off the radio because suddenly I didn't need any company. I could hardly drive the twisting road for gawping at the mighty sight of sea and mountains come together in such powerful concert. "My God! My God!" was the only reasonable exclamation, and I kept exclaiming it as I rounded bend after bend and the spectacle kept getting better. The mountains along the coast could have been shot like foam from an aerosol can. They rush, bubbly, frothy, looping madly down the coast, lightly decked with green or frosty-grey cover, high above the surf. Giant rocks, broken, lay scattered in the boiling white water. From the rocks, the ocean backs way, way out to the flat horizon in successively darker bands of blue. I have never seen country so strong, so broad-shouldered, and I whipped through it on a road hung halfway between water and sky, on perilous cliffs, spanning gigantic gorges, rushing through sudden stands of sweet-smelling eucalyptus and topless, towering redwoods.

There is no proper town of Big Sur, but soon after a road

sign suggests that a town is coming up, there does appear a Richfield gas station with its big yellow sign, a band of tourist cottages and a fly-specked bar and restaurant with a message pinned to the screen door barring beards, hippies, and bare feet. At this point you are a long way from comfort stations. How comfortable not to have a beard or bare feet, or be otherwise noticeable.

Ten miles farther on, I passed Nepenthe, an eagle's lair of a restaurant hanging high above the ocean, full of tourists who scoff up Ambrosia-burgers and gin martinis and buy psychedelic posters in the basement shop adjoining the dovecote. I began to worry that I had passed Esalen, that one of the few tiny mailboxes I had seen, standing absurdly, suburbanly alone against the drop-away cliffs, had been the only identifying marker. I also began to worry about arriving at Esalen, Episcopal connection or no Episcopal connection. I was scared, but I didn't know it at the time.

At length I came on a wide, shelflike promontory on the ocean side of the road, and a sign marked "ESALEN—BY RESERVATION ONLY." Below lay a complex of low redwood buildings, on a descending series of terraces, facing a kidney-shaped swimming pool and the edge of the cliff. Beyond the cliff were only ocean and sky. The glare from the water cast the main lodge into deep shadow, but as I approached, I could make out on the fringes and by the porch a most unusual collection of silhouettes. There were what appeared to be Indian women in long flowing gowns, and long-haired Cherokees in high-brimmed, feathered, five-gallon hats. I made out a young Indian chopping at the soil with a hoe, and on drawing closer saw that he was just Harry Highschool, stripped to the waist and wearing a beaded band across his brow. Though I liked to think of myself as a moderately swinging square, I suffered immediate anxiety. "Hippies," I breathed to myself, alarmed.

At the desk were three very pretty and thoroughly distracted young girls in Indian Paisley print gowns. "Atcheson," said one, as if it were a rather fanciful lyric. "Atcheson . . . I think you're in number eight. Now where *is* that key?" Nobody appeared disposed to help me, and I found my room by wandering around. It was a dreary room, despite its commanding view of the ocean—all glass door and front, and no other windows at all, so that from the headboard of the bed, against the rear wall, I seemed to be backed into a long, low cave, defending my three-button suit against the elemental multitudes.

God knows I felt defensive, and hostile—disliked and lonely. What a way to run a joint, I thought. From two o'clock until well after eleven that night, not one person spoke to me. I wandered around, I looked at the pool with nobody in it, I looked at the sky, I retreated to my room. I went to the dining room at dinnertime. The meal was good but I didn't like having to chew there, alone, in the middle of a crowd, all of whom seemed to know everybody but me.

At nine o'clock, after many collective confusions and delays, the weekend seminar began in an annex to the dining room. Our instructor was to be Magda Proskauer, a physiotherapist, once a student of Jung, who teaches body awareness and breathing therapy in San Francisco. What, I wondered fearfully, might body awareness be? It turned out to be an initially simple business of all of us, twenty-five or so, lying down on the floor and listening to Magda Proskauer. She is a tiny, lively lady of a certain age, with a frightful

German accent but many intriguing, fascinating things to say. One of the things she suggested is that we are not in touch with our bodies. Many of us, for example, do not wholly believe that our bodies will breathe without our control. I had never thought about that in my life, but I realized that it is certainly true of me that *I* do all the breathing around here. When Magda suggests that one might exhale and just wait for the body to take the next breath, some of her students have been known to panic utterly.

Later that night I went down to the baths, which are more or less segregated by sex during the day, but from twilight onward, coed. Those who are now salivating for an orgiastic sex scene had best look elsewhere. That is not to suggest that sex scenes could not or do not develop in the baths, but I would not know about that. It didn't happen while I was there, though many deliciously pleasant things did, and the baths were far and away my favorite spot at Esalen. They are, perhaps, a sort of symbol of the acceptance of awareness, of honesty, which seems to me to be at the center of the Esalen experience. It is good to walk down a path to a terrace, closed on three sides and roofed, but open to the sea and sky, to take off your clothes and sink into one of several wide, deep tubs full of the hot spring water that flows ceaselessly down the mountain toward the sea. It is good to be able to do that with other people, alone with them or together with them as you feel. I went to the baths many times and it seemed to me that it was a uniquely private place. I was very tranquil there, and happy. I could soak in the hot spring water, and sit and smoke and talk with others, or simply be with the sky and the sea and me. I thought it was great.

The Proskauer seminar went on through the weekend, and so did the regular life of Esalen. The mornings started with *T'ai Chi ch'uan* exercises by the pool—a series of antique, balletic postures developed in China. I felt rather foolish and exposed at first, performing these wide, sweeping movements with all nature looking on. I wonder what I thought the trees saw. I met a few of the Resident Fellows, people quite various in age and apparent stability, who stay at Esalen for nine months and engage in a constant "encounter" with one another, trying to be quite specifically honest with themselves and each other All the Time. I liked them. In the Proskauer exercises, I lay on an open deck, getting in touch with my lower back, with my right leg, with my head, beginning to get surprisingly voluptuous messages back, concentrating on my body and finding that it liked me well enough to reward my interest with quite the most euphoric feeling of relaxation and well-being that I have ever experienced. With Magda I learned to give up the controls I tend to keep so rigidly on my Self, to let go, to allow my Self to unsnarl the knots my tensions tie me up with. It may sound nuts but it's all very simple stuff and I, who had always considered myself the original relaxed, easy-going guy, needed it badly.

In this self-absorption, I guess I stopped pushing so hard, thrusting myself forward so assertively, and at that moment experience began to flow toward me quite naturally. I wasn't out there, punching like Sluggo any more, and things and people came to me. A couple of very good people, who try all the time to get used to not lying, invited me to try the same. It is the most scary thing in the world, to tell the truth. The truth is absolutely nitroglycerin, and if you don't know how dangerous it can be, you just don't know what the truth is. Who are you? What do you feel now? What do you want now? Honest answers to questions like that can change everything, can ruin or redirect lives. I found I lied a lot while trying to answer those questions. I could hear the lies in my mouth and I hated it but I didn't know how to get to the truth. And then after thirty minutes of babbling such guck as even I could scarcely believe, I guess I tapped the keg where I am. And I was saying things about myself I'd never heard before. Scary, boy. I felt like a child.

In this condition, I found I could be with people more really than I had ever been before. I was angry and impatient with myself—how could I have lived to be thirty-three years old and know, acknowledge so little about me?—but I could appreciate somebody else more directly, more richly. I remember a conversation in the baths, with a very hairy, well-spoken hippie. He said he had not known how much hate there was in the world until he let his beard grow. In San Jose one day, an angry man came up to him on the street and thrust two dollar bills into his fist. "Here, you filthy thing," he said. "Go get a haircut." The boy said, "Thank you, but I don't really want to get my hair cut. May I use the money for food?" And the angry man snatched the money back again.

Later that week, at Davenport, north on the coast, I was reminded of that story while having breakfast in one of those clean, spruce, friendly eateries you find only in California. I heard the two girls behind the counter talking. "Grace," says one, "you know those two nice-looking boys that was in here a while ago, that looked so neat and clean, hitchhiking from Fort Ord? Well, do you know they went out to hitchhike and they was a bunch of hippies out there, and somebody went and picked up them hippies and left them nice-looking boys standing there." Grace said, "Well, I think people pick up the hippies just to find out what makes 'em tick." "Tick, hell," says the first girl, "they don't tick. Hell, they don't even rattle when you kick 'em."

That would be a funny story if it weren't so tragic. So would all the incredible, blocking, anesthetizing things we do to ourselves, if it weren't so desperately sad. The kids know that there is something deeply wrong and dishonest about the way we live, and their rebellion is neither idle nor foolish. They want to say yes when they feel yes and no when they feel no. They want to be alive and they are right to want that.

On my last night at Esalen, I went down to the baths at sunset. I watched the fantastic clouds roil around and saw the sun put on a pyrotechnical show that was better than a private screening of *King of Kings*. And then the sun flattened straight out on the horizon and a storm came up and darkness covered the earth. Somebody had left behind one stubby candle and it guttered away behind me, flaming out in a puff of wind, lighting up feebly otherwise, under a hanging pot of ferns. For a change I was alone there. I steamed luxuriously in one of the big tubs, then climbed out and sat, naked, warm, relaxed, gazing out and down on the black water, the rocks, the crashing waves and swirling white foam. A very light cool rain began to fall, and my body liked it. It was just a patter of raindrops, sprinkling on a happy man. There was no tension in me—only deep repose, bone-deep—as I considered whether I could go on saying no, and yes.

the esalen copout

scarcely had I wafted myself out of Esalen and up the coast highway than I began to make a damned nuisance of myself with my wife, my family, and my friends. I proselytized like crazy on all fronts, bore a maddening, saintly smile much of the time, and alienated just about everybody.

There was the first phone call home, when in my euphoria I forgot that New York is later than San Francisco, and roused my wife out of a deep sleep at three in the morning.

"Huh?" she said, and there I was on the other coast, purring in that whisper-quiet Esalen voice that I had found The Answer, that I had stumbled among the Beautiful People, that we were going to stop *Lying,* that This was IT. "It is?" she said, weakly. "What is?"

She also said would I *please* speak up, she couldn't hear a word I was saying. Not much later in the month, she was asking me to please shut up, and I do not blame her in the least.

For reasons I do not yet clearly understand, I found myself eager to sell Esalen. Instead of exploring and working on with the hangups of my own life, I wanted to get out there and hustle the Good News. In fact, the Good News has spread very nicely, all by itself, all over the country. The only people it may never reach are the poor victims I talked to.

Even the preceding piece for *Holiday* was, by a very considerable margin, a copout. I didn't have much space, true; but also, I was worried about what *Holiday* would buy, and I was even more worried about giving the story the right Packaging. If I didn't make the Esalen thing attractive and palatable and unscary, not only would people think I was crazy, they would think Esalen was crazy.

So I withheld certain events and encounters that were of major importance to my four days at Esalen, and the result was that many readers could not see what in the world had happened to so change my life. As the piece stands, it's provocative enough to gain attention, but it just doesn't tell the story.

I omitted, for example, my first decisive act after checking into my room at Esalen, which was to leave At Once. The whole place bugged me terribly, and I needed a drink, and at two o'clock in the afternoon the Esalen wine and beer bar is shut. So I drove up the steep road to the coast highway, determined to retrace my route to Nepenthe for a martini.

The highway at the entrance to Esalen was thronged with hitchhikers, most of them California gypsies in ponchos and floppy hats and long hair. Well of course I didn't want to pick up any of *them*—but just down the road I saw an extraordinarily neat hitchhiker. He had a beard, all right, but he also had button-down collar and cuffs. Wow. A straight gypsy.

So I picked him up. I hoped to get a little background dope on Esalen, and I had chosen well. Fred (he said his name was) was a nine-month Fellow. He was on his way to Monterey to lead a twenty-four-hour encounter group, which was a job some of the Fellows could do to pick up extra dough during the stint at Esalen. He used language I couldn't always follow, not being into the jargon, like T-grouper and the like, but I managed. Also I found that he was a very pleasant guy and I was easy and relaxed in his company. I got no vibration from him that he despised me for my jacket and tie and short haircut and Hertz Rent-a-Car. We just talked and I learned stuff and it was okay.

I turned in at Nepenthe and Fred went off to hitch a ride farther north. And after a drink and a hamburger I went back to Esalen and felt awful the rest of the day, and apprehensive about what was to come. But I got through the first session with Magda okay, despite being annoyed at having to sit on the floor and tell my name and where I was from and what I was there for, like a goddam kindergartener (boy, I was really hostile). And I was just having a beer and deciding to go down to the baths when in walked Fred. That's funny, I thought. He said he'd be leading a twenty-four-hour encounter in Monterey and here he is again.

Well, it had all been got wrong. He'd hitchhiked all the way there, and had got the date wrong, or maybe they'd got the date wrong, and nobody was sure how it was but anyway *wrong,* so he'd hitchhiked back. I thought, God what a waste of time that a phone call could have cured. But I was having my first lesson among the Beautiful and the Free. Time and schedules and phones and easy solutions just don't get much attention. And clearly Fred was not in the least unhappy or showing signs of wear. On the contrary, he was delighted to be back and to see me, and pleased that the guy who had given him a lift had consented to come into Esalen and see around, and he then introduced me to this cat, a very pleasant and amiable young man from L.A., who looked as puzzled then as I had felt earlier in the afternoon.

We bullshat for a time, and then agreed to go down to the baths, where I had not yet been. It was dark night, and the air was chilly, but there was a big happy crowd, and we took our clothes off and got into one of the big square tubs for scores of people, and talked there a long time, but I honestly do not remember about what, except that Fred laid more on us about Esalen, and being open, and telling the truth. Then his friend and erstwhile benefactor, whose name I don't remember but shall here call Norman, remarked that he had to leave because it was late at night and he would have a long drive to L.A.

Oh no, we protested, he mustn't attempt the cliff roads at this hour, a sack must be found. I knew well enough that

I had a single room with one double bed and one single bed, but I wasn't about to volunteer if Fred had some safer idea. But he didn't, it turned out, and I heard myself inviting this amiable but perfect stranger to share my private room. So that was settled, and we dressed and walked back up to the residential complex, Fred departing for his room at some juncture along the dark path.

Norman and I went into my room, but without turning on the lights I could tell something was amiss. Snores. Loud, snorting snores. As my eyes adjusted to the inside blackness, I could see the true perfidy of the place. Here I'm paying for a single room and they have blithely moved somebody else in with me, and there he lies, snoring his head off in *my* extra bed. So what to do with Norman. "Norman," says I, ruing it, "you see how it is. You are welcome to share my double bed but of course that is a ghastly proposition, and the best I can offer you."

So we shared, Norman climbing warily in from one side and me from the other, both of us clinging to the mattress edge for fear we should *touch* each other, me thinking "He's queer," him thinking "He's queer." Of course we spent a sleepless night. And was I ever glad to hear, by dawn's early light, the sinuous sounds of a flute, which indicated that we could abandon our bed of indecision and terror, and go to breakfast.

Norman stayed half the day, sitting in on the morning sessions with Proskauer. We worked on the terrace in the sunshine, doing a lot of lying about and feeling our backs, and there was a rush of monarch butterflies in the air over our heads, and I liked it extremely. Before lunch, Norman asked me to hear parts of his book manuscript (for like all young men he was writing an autobiographical novel only lightly disguised), and I listened and applauded. After lunch he left with many stated regrets, and Fred and I resumed the Proskauer experience. At one point we were to choose partners and sit back to back and see what we might feel stirring in the other back. Fred and I were partners, and it seemed to me that he had a hell of a busy back. It was full of messages; not certain of ground rules, I thought I might be misunderstanding. But the touch, even at that rudimentary level, seemed to me unmistakable. There was something happening between our backs. I wondered where our heads fit into all this.

That evening Fred had some prior commitment and did not come to Magda's session, which turned out to be rather more verbal than previously. There was talk, debate, argument, and I found myself afterward exchanging views rather heatedly with a very attractive, wide-eyed girl in a black leotard who said she was from Palo Alto, was named Jill, and was also a nine-month Fellow. I liked her so well that I invited her into the wine and beer bar for a glass of wine, and after some stammering about, she accepted.

Jill had been praising the work of a man named Alexander Lowen, a New York psychotherapist who had done a long seminar at Esalen. She said he liked to put the human body into stressful (but not painful) positions, so that under the stress of the posture, the tensions would sort of shake and roll their way out. She showed me a couple of the postures and I was horrified at how torturous they looked, but she and some other Fellows there assured me that they weren't.

So we talked some more about Lowen, and then about Jill's experience thus far at Esalen, which she admitted she found very difficult. She said people would ask her how she was, and at Esalen that is a *profound* question, and she could never sort out exactly how she did feel at any given moment. She said that twenty-four-hour encounter, thirty-one days a month, nine months of the year, was a frightening prospect for her. And she spoke of Fritz Perls, the acknowledged inventor of Gestalt therapy, the resident Esalen guru whose thinking had so informed the whole thrust of the institute. I had at that time not met Perls, but I had seen him stalking about, greatly white-bearded, over seventy, and still bursting with vigor, in a blue terry-cloth jumpsuit, like some Viennese pixie from an altered North Pole. "I can't get close to Fritz," Jill said. "He's the only person here I'm really scared of."

Which having been said, who should enter the bar and walk straight over to our table and sit down but Fritz Perls. "Oh *hi*," said Jill, in a shrill, unnatural voice. "Aren't you tired? I thought you'd be tired after your trip."

Long pause from Perls. Then: "I vas tired, but I couldn't slip. Zo I came up here to play chess. For me, chess is the zame as Nirvana."

"Wow," says I, "I guess I'd better take up chess."

Pause from Perls. "For me," he said, "Nirvana is easier."

"Oh shit," says I to myself.

Perls paused, and went on. "Today," he said, "I vas in zuh Haight, in a haus fur coffee. Und I vas zeeink, und I vas beink, und it vas beautiful."

Jill brightened. "How was the weather in San Francisco?" she asked.

Pause. "Vhat?"

"I said," urged Jill, "how was the weather in the city? It

was beautiful here, just gorgeous. I thought maybe it was nice in San Francisco?"

Pause. "I haf not zeen Zan Franzisco in two years."

At the time, I could not appreciate the perfection of Fritz's no-bullshit life style. I just saw Jill writhing there in a paroxysm of frustration, and I got very masculine and rescued her, which may well have been the wrong thing.

"Well," says I. "We really must be going. Come on, Jill, time to make it out of here, ha-ha, see you later, Mr. Perls." And we split.

I was bound for the baths, had my towel over my shoulder in fact, and said to Jill on the terrace, "Are you going to the baths?"

And Jill said, "Well no, not really." And at Esalen that is *so* obtuse and confused an answer that it would never make it, not even with me, who had been there less than two days. I mean, you either *are* going to the baths or you are *not* going to the baths, but either way, you say it and you do it and all this bullshit will not wash. But I am polite and was raised right so I held on. And Jill said that in fact she'd like to lend me a book by Alexander Lowen, so why didn't I come up to her room and get it.

Hmmmm. Does Atcheson cop out? Is she inviting me to something greater than a book? Do I hope she is, or do I hope she isn't?

Dick and Jill are sitting in Jill's room on her double-bed coverlet, eating apples. Jill has given me Lowen's book but we are still talking and I am trying to figure out what Jill expects me to do now. No word of my wife and multitudinous children has passed my lips, just in case she should expect me to do something I might want to do, even though

I am by no means sure that I will want to do it if the occasion should present itself.

I ask Jill what this twenty-four-hour encounter is really like. Not lying *ever?* How to achieve such a thing? She says that the Fellows have a couple of organized sessions of encounter every week, and work on one another. And she reveals that she has come less far than most people in openness and honesty. She says again that she never knows how she feels, and when people ask she is stumped for an answer. And I say yeah, but what's it like?

So Jill explains that the important questions appear to be: Who are you? What do you want right now? What do you need right now? And I ask, like a lummox, how long is now? Jill says huh? I say, I mean, how long? Is now going to be three minutes or three hours or three days? And what happens afterward?

Jill says, naturally, that now is *now,* this minute. Like, she says, for example, what do you need this minute?

And I thought, well, I guess I need to kiss this girl, just to find out what *else* is going to happen. So I leaned forward and kissed Jill on the cheek.

"I'm glad you did it that way," she said, accepting the kiss. "I don't think I could handle anything else right now."

Whew, I thought, thank God, now I know we are *not* going to go to bed. And oddly, that knowledge freed me a bit for the next questions she put, which were, of course, Who Are You? What Do You Need? and What Do You Want? I tried to answer, but I could not. I had no practice in the Now, a concept I densely could not understand, and I was so constipated with standard answers to those alarming questions that I got nowhere at all. Finally, by some

fluke, Jill asked, Why do you write? And that one got me.
I lied for a long while, attributing my writing urge to everything under the sun, including Mother and the Flag. But
finally I was telling the truth, the facts as they had come to
be.

"I write because I want everyone to love me," I said. "I
don't even know who 'they' are and I don't care about them,
but I want them to care about *me*. I want them to drive by
my house and say, 'There's the house of Richard Atcheson,
the famous writer. You know, the one with the lovely wife,
the charming children, the three cars."

And hearing that, I died a bit inside. Because that was
not why I had always wanted to write. That was nothing
to do with what had motivated me. That was *shit*. But that
was, still, true, and I had not looked at that or been aware
of it.

Once I got talking in this pure strain, I talked plenty,
wincing the while, and I did not leave Jill until after dawn.
And went back to my room, and while my roommate snored
on, watched the sunrise and thought more about how I had
lied to myself, and wondered what in the world I was going
to do about it.

That morning I was a Talking Fool. I just purely could
not shut up. I had a long talk with Fred, and long talks
with I don't know who, and a long verbose lunch with
several Fellows, burbling on about my ignorance of myself,
and what a mind blower it was to find out that you've been
doing dumb stuff you didn't even know you were doing, for
reasons you've never even *noticed*. And while I talked, some
girl at the table started to weep very quietly, and another
Fellow put her hand over hers to comfort her, but nobody

suggested that the girl leave or I shut up. And later Fred told me that the girl and her husband, under the pressure of being nine-month Fellows, were beginning to sort out their relationship and probably would split up, and that I sounded, to her, like her.

Somewhere in the middle of that, it was time for me to go for my first Esalen massage. I was pretty paranoid about this, too. People had told me that I had to get a massage, that it was central to the Esalen experience, but I was scared of it. The techniques were said to be built on Javanese massage, which is used as an aid to meditation, and is both erotic and intellectual at once, and I was afraid that that was putting an awful lot into a little rubdown. But I went down to the sacred baths at the time appointed and, heart pounding, asked for Gail, the girl who had signed up to massage me. (Fred had unwittingly terrified me even further by confiding, in advance, that he had asked Gail not to wear anything while massaging me, which is the custom for Esalen regulars, but that she had refused, saying that I was a writer and there was no telling what scandal I might publish about *that*.)

So Gail was there, and quite naked, and quite beautiful, and quite matter-of-fact. She was hosing down a section of the floor, and broke off to say she thought I should take a long hot soak, and just let the tensions roll off in the water. She said she would do the same, and then we would both meet in the massage room when we were ready. I did all she had told me, and when I felt ready I went on into the massage room, and sure enough, here she came too. But now she wore a black leotard.

The massage room is part of the baths complex, and

hangs out above the cliffs over the Pacific, and the water pounds and surges there below you night and day. There was a slight chill in the room, but Gail had lighted an electric fire, she had candles burning here and there, and had spread a sheet on the massage table. I got up and lay down naked on the table, and Gail busied herself about the place, and with my eyes closed all I knew was the tap and clink and shuffle of her movements, until I sensed that she was standing behind my head.

In that quiet, gentle Esalen voice she said, "I'm going to start with some head work, and when I finish I'll do some more head work if I can. So you just relax and be with my hands, and just one thing . . . please don't talk."

I don't think anyone could properly explain the significance of that massage. I had got a glimmer of an idea of what the body is capable of, from the seminar with Magda. I had learned a bit about breathing, and I found that I could follow, with my breath, wherever Gail's hands were. I found that at her urging I could allow her to lift my head, and move it about. That doesn't, in words, sound like anything. But I guarantee that if you can allow someone else to have your head, it is one of the most buoyant and liberating experiences in life.

It wasn't long, of course, before I was aware that I had the most blissful, undemanding erection. At that moment I heard Gail's voice: "Don't worry. That's expected." *Expected,* I thought. Goddamn unavoidable. And didn't mind. The massage went on for three hours. Those hands taught me things about my body that I'd never dreamed, and the erotic content was by no means the most of it. The experience was principally intellectual, but I have always lamely explained it away by saying that it was as if my body were a ripe fruit, being burst open. With wisdom. And love.

I came away grateful, and a wiser, quieter man. But I can't tell you exactly why.

Late that afternoon, Fred came by and suggested a walk. At Esalen, when somebody invites you for a walk, he means a walk. And if you say no, I don't feel like a walk, you are not understood to be saying I don't love you, I reject you, you are no fucking good. You are understood to be saying, simply, that you don't want to go for a walk.

But I did want to go for a walk, and so I did. With Fred. We walked along the coast highway for a long time, digging the gigantic ocean and the sky exploding with clouds. And I talked a little bit about the massage. But mostly we didn't say anything.

Then we drove to Nepenthe and had a martini at the bar. And we talked a bit about the Proskauer session on the terrace, and the backs. I said I thought I had detected more, in our backs, than just sensory awareness. He said that I had. And so had he. Hmmmmmm.

That's just about all we ever said about that. Fred was more disturbed than I was, in funny ways. I had had homosexual encounters in my life before, and told him so. But he never had, and he was having trouble sorting this thing out, and trying to see how it fit, if at all, into his assumptions about himself, and what he was learning. He may indeed still be trying to assimilate an experience that came to us when we were looking in totally opposite directions.

What it meant to me, under the impetus of Esalen honesty, was that I had to confront my own bisexuality, because it was a fact. I had never acknowledged it; I had married, presumably I had *chosen*. But in fact there was a whole side of my life that I was pretending wasn't there. To live bluntly and honestly with Who I Am meant to live with my own sexuality, and to acknowledge capacities in myself that exist, dormant or animated, in everyone. It doesn't go down well at the country club, and it sure plays hell with the job, but on the other hand, why should the country club and the job determine Who I Am? That's crazy.

It was my wife who got the brunt of the consequences of this, of course. I insisted, on return home, with a very evangelical zeal, that we examine, each to each, just who the other was married to. At my insistence, we put all the kangaroos out on the coffee table and boxed every one of them insensible. Needless to say, it just about wrecked our marriage. And in fact, I guess that, so long as it lasts, which I still hope is forever, our marriage will list to port like a torpedoed P-T boat. But, my wife willing, it will be a real marriage, and not one of those charades you can witness any night at Longchamps, when the husband and wife come in and order and eat and go out again, and have not said a single word throughout. At Esalen I conceived the determination that I would not, if I could help it, live with lies any more. And I'm still trying.

Thus this addendum to the Esalen experience. This is how it was, and why it was important. And I am aware of the possible consequences. The usual equation is that, if you tell people the truth, you will be in their power. I did tell this story to one acquaintance, a man who has been writing a book about homosexuality. He listened warmly to my tale and went away. And then I heard from a mutual friend that he was telling around that I am not only queer but crazy.

That may be. But events do come full circle, and I was amused the other day to be called by a publisher, who said that this man had applied for a job, and what could I say about him? I mentioned that he had been writing this major study of homosexuality for the past two years. "Ah," said the publisher. "Is he . . . uh . . . involved?"

mendocino, village of the lost

count on me to pick my Moments with an unerring instinct for disaster. I showed up in San Francisco to do a piece on San Francisco State University on the very eve of what later became nationally known as its Troubles. But I had no inkling of what was brewing. My baby sister was a senior there just then; I knew the place was reported to be the most exciting streetcar college in the country; they had a fine faculty and eighteen thousand nifty kids enrolled and they had been doing some risky, promising things in educational reform, and I wanted to write about what was happening.

But the story never worked out. I found my sister residing on Diamond Street in the Slough of Despond, otherwise known as the State of Suspended Animation. She and all her friends, who had seemed so full of life when I last visited them, were sitting around enervated, pessimistic about State, and deeply bearish about the whole proposition of studies and academic degrees. And the minute I put my toe on the campus greensward, the whole place erupted in riot and rebellion over issues I never could sort out; every individual and group published manifestoes against every other individual and group, and all positions changed at five-minute intervals, and all I could make out was that the cops were breaking student heads on the public streets, which I did not care for. Nobody appeared to be in any greater command than I was; indeed, the president of the college one day abruptly flew the coop (whether he resigned or was asked to leave was also a subject for argument) and hopped a plane for Addis Ababa, which is a destination I could not have invented for him if I were a fiction writer with the imagination of William Burroughs.

The hell with this, I said to myself. If the president of the college seeks calm in Africa, and he a bright, progressive scholar and the Gary Goodguy of American education, this is no place for me. So that night I went to my last student party (a very chaste affair on Twin Peaks, memorable only because of the line my hostess greeted me with, which was, "Gee, we're all out of grass; would you like some opium?"), and I sought advice on where I could go that would be, if less distant and exotic than Ethiopia, an agreeable contrast to the Sturm und Drang of State.

Now asking college students about travel is like asking the starving multitudes of Calcutta what they like for breakfast. Nobody has any dough to squander on travel and, for my sister at least, a trip around the block is a pretty heady experience; but there were kids at the party who had used their thumbs to cover much of the coast to north and south, and they said that the country in either direction was terrific. I had been south before, along the Big Sur, but never north, so I decided to strike out next day for the Russian River country, for the logging camps and curious, under-populated villages of this silent, empty coastal wilderness.

I don't think there is any more hopeful, optimistic way to start a trip than to cross the Golden Gate Bridge from San Francisco into Marin County. Halfway across I risked a glance backward at the city, gleaming white against a deep blue sky. Below me in the bay, hundreds of sailboats skimmed across the water. Ahead of me, the gold and green hills of Tiburon rose up in the sunshine, and the wispy fingers of a lingering mist floated in among them as if in rehearsal for a Chinese brush painting.

While most of the northbound traffic swept onto a broad expressway, I made my escape into Route 1, the two-lane coastal highway that winds with every ripple of the shoreline all the way to Fort Bragg, over a range of rugged mountain slopes forested in redwoods. This is the coast you used to be able to see from the air, before the days of the jets, when flying out of San Francisco for Hawaii. I remember that from the air it always looked vaguely un-American,

Oriental, as if the journey to the inscrutable East truly began at the western edge of the Pacific. On the ground it was just as eerie, and very hard to drive. The road twists along in tight turns and steep grades, occasionally domesticated when it rushes through a two-block Christian town, but instantly Dionysian when it dashes out crazily into the wilderness again. Great rocks lie abandoned in the surf all along, rocks in the shape of sails and castles, rocks with the conformation of dinosaurs and giant crabs, the proper denizens of nightmare and madness. Landward, the alien hills bulge up rounded and smooth, as if patted into place by a child's soft palm. In places, some desperate farmer will have planted a stone fence to mark his property line, and it will rise, sunken but straight as a die, creasing the silken side of a hill like the track of a fingernail across a human thigh.

As I drove along, goggling at all this, I passed many a hairy youth by the roadside, but for the first hour I didn't pick anybody up because I was enjoying myself too much. In the rest of the country I'd never dream of picking anybody up anyway, sure I'd get a Bonnie-and-Clyde hole in the back of my head, but the California coast is a different story—especially in those wild, lonely stretches, where nature seems so hostile that people are friendly out of necessity. Anyway, in this part of the world it is well known that the college generation has hit the road without any resource except the good will of drivers; the risk is small, and the line of winsome youths along the shoulder gets to be a reproach after a while. Finally I did pull over and pick up a barefoot boy with an awful lot of hair, and he thanked me very warmly for doing so. "I was really worried," he told me. "There I was at that little crossroads, and a guy pulled up and I thought he wanted to give me a ride, but he only cursed me. Then he pulled across to that filling station and he kept pointing at me and I thought I was in trouble. I happen to be a light middleweight in college and I could probably whip his ass, but not without any shoes on."

I asked the boy where he was going, and he said, "Oh, I don't know, somewhere up here about ten miles." So we rode along, admiring the countryside, until I noticed a blond hairy youth stepping out of the wilderness into the road up ahead, and the boy said, "I guess this is it," and he thanked me and was out of the car consorting with the blond boy, and I went my way, wondering how the hell they had ever hoped to make this magical meeting in the middle of no-place, and what mystical role I had unwittingly played in it. It had all been so fey that I picked up the next kid I saw, though he was a very different looking sort of kid, his collar all buttoned down and his hair short enough to win him a Lions Club scholarship—no doubt about it, the most dangerous kind of hitchhiker there is. But he was also pleasant company, and his enthusiasm for the country knew no bounds. He was carrying a bedroll and a Modern Library edition of Thoreau, and he told me he was bound for a gulch up ahead where he planned to stay for three or four days and "find some peace." I asked him what he was going to eat in the midst of all this peace. "I don't really know," he said, "but I guess I'll meet somebody, or something will turn up. I have these friends who are probably coming up here in a couple of days, and there's this girl after me—

that's really why I'm up here, I'm trying to get away from her, but she'll figure it out and she'll probably be up—and if not, well, uh, you know."

I did not know, but I didn't press it. When I was in parochial school, the nuns used to tell us that God would provide, and I figure that this kid was on to something very like what motivated the sisters of the Congregation of Divine Providence, except that, obviously, he really meant it. (No rector, no parish, no Knights of the Holy Sepulchre dwell in the gulch this kid was bound for.) The kid asked me where I was going and I said that ultimately I hoped to hit Mendocino, where I was told that if you squint it could be a true Maine fishing village, on account of having been built by forty-niners from Maine who failed to find gold and went back to fishing again. "Oh yeah," he said, "Mendocino is a groovy town. A lot of people run off to Mendocino, live up in the woods, stuff like that. I know a guy there from State, Ph.D. and all, got it last year, just junked it all and went up there to live. When you get there, ask for Mike. He's got a dog and a beard. They probably know him."

The country got wilder and emptier. Vast, undulating moors stretched toward the sea. Fields of sweet clover lay purple and still among the wildly waving tall grasses, and along the road, miles of picket fence ran a spindly, uncertain course, betrayed by washouts into buckled breaks and improbable Spanish fans. It was here that my passenger bailed out, itching to walk down toward the sea. "Good luck," he said, hurrying to vault the fence. "Hope you like Mendocino —too many people there for me."

I didn't make Mendocino that night, because I got scared. I know it's silly, but I was low on gas and the road got much worse, all blind corners and thousands of feet to fall over the edge, and goats wandering into the highway. The evening sun settled down on the rim of the ocean and absolutely blistered my eyes. I couldn't see properly, I had at least another two hours of driving, and I had a great vision of myself stranded out of gas on an empty road where I hadn't seen another car for at least an hour.

When I reached Fort Ross, the old Russian fort that stands gaunt and rough-sided on a wind-swept hill, I wandered around in the chill breeze, liking the rugged, weathered redwood palisades but feeling lonely and regretful about being there all by myself. A few miles farther on, I swept past the only motel I had seen on the coast, a commercial-looking outfit with a martini glass outlined in neon, but by then I was brave again and thought I'd carry on, at least as far as the Sea Ranch. I didn't know what the Sea Ranch was, but there had been signs for it and I took it to be some kind of inn. When I rounded a bend and saw the silhouette of its first buildings, standing sharp-edged against the setting sun, I remembered it at once from pictures I had seen—a collection of condominiums crouched in the moors at the edge of the cliff, roofs raked away from the sea breeze like windbreaks, sided with natural redwood or cedar shakes, as much a part of the landscape as the rocks or the grass. And empty. Built and ready, but shut. Thirsty, hungry and a little anxious, I turned tail and hurried back to that neon martini glass.

The bar was full of locals—carpenters, construction workers—who had come down out of the hills to curse the wilderness, and the Sea Ranch, and all the works of God and man. They spoke of how the Sea Ranch, an ever-proliferating enterprise, would someday stretch its cottages and condominiums over eighteen miles of the moors. They complained that they were in an empty, godforsaken place, with nothing to do but drink. They compared lies about who had worked hardest, for the least money, and how fast they had driven on the twisting highway when drunk, and who had had the biggest crack-up. One carpenter even told of wanting to move on to Klamath Falls, "a real town." You could tell that they really loved that country.

Next morning, the air was mountain-cool, the sun bright, and the sea sparkling white through the cypresses lining the cliff. I moved on, past the Sea Ranch and its pregnant pastures, its lots and roads marked in the high grass with white-tipped sticks, into empty country again. Beaches where I paused were sandy-grey and stretched for miles, and not a soul was on them. The sand dunes were carpeted with all kinds of flowering creepers and prickly, reedy grass, and below them lay tons and tons of drifted logs, sea-polished, sun-bleached, and tossed at mad random to the back of the beach. Here and there, where the sand had drifted away, parts of a buried redwood log shone copper-red and soft as sealskin. It was a finish we will never see on redwood picnic tables.

Having dawdled, I didn't get to Mendocino until late morning. I rounded a bend, and saw the town across a deep bay, sitting up on a high spit of land, and it was love at first sight. Despite my preparation, it was still a shock to see a little Maine town transported entire to the northern California coast, where it has no business to be. And other sources of association rose quickly to the surface, for Mendocino has been used in many movies, notably *East of Eden* and *The Russians Are Coming, The Russians Are Coming,* and I had loved the look of things in both those films. The white-steepled churches, the little gingerbread cottages lined up snug behind picket fences and rows of roses and snapdragons, the empty, grassy lots where abandoned houses rotted, fell down, and were carried off—that is Mendocino. I remembered James Dean wandering those dusty streets, past those occasional cottages, in search of his mother. And the cast of *The Russians Are Coming, Etc.,* running helter-skelter through those same streets in comic panic. I was amazed to find that I knew this town very well.

Of course, it is not pristine. The artsy and the craftsy have moved in, and Mendocino is becoming just a little cute. But the fishing and the logging that gave the town its reason for existence have long since died off, and their passing just about killed the place. The only hope Mendocino has is that it is most improbably there, and the fact of its existence will draw the tourist dollar in sufficient quantity to keep the town alive. And the fanciful, lighthearted, way-out shops making their appearance on Main Street, and the art and sculpture galleries opening up in the old cottages, are an essential part of Mendocino's lease on life.

As I wandered around, I found one of the special curiosities to be Gallery Fair, an amalgam of picture gallery and candy kitchen operated by a gent named John Storm. Mr. Storm also directs the local play-acting society, and uses the rear of his establishment, a former lodge hall, for rehearsals. When I entered his parlor he was sitting, elderly, white-haired, and elegant, in a high-back Victorian rocker. He looked up from his paper to greet me. "Good afternoon," he said, the words rolling off his tongue after the manner of

John Barrymore in *Twentieth Century*. "Do you *know* the house?"

"Uh, no," I stammered.

"Very well," he said. "The paintings and sculpture are Up Those Stairs. The kitchen is at the rear on this floor. If you require anything, I Am At Your Service." I wandered through the upstairs gallery, then returned downstairs and tiptoed past Mr. Storm, who was then on the phone ("I know, dear, but Tuesday is the only day I can possibly meet with the cast this week"), into the kitchen. It was the perfect evocation of Grandma's nookery—warm and spicy with the aroma of freshly baked cookies, a tin kettle boiling on the stove and a stock pot simmering. Mouth watering, but reluctant to disturb the tranquillity of the scene, or Mr. Storm's plans for his rehearsal, I tiptoed past him again and, with a wave, went out to seek a hamburger.

Later I wandered into a sort of modified head shop on Main Street, a place just opened, called the Ultimate Remedy. Dean and Kim Davis, proprietors, are a young couple who have escaped the hurly-burly of Fresno for the comparative quiet of Mendocino and mercantile enterprise. Their shop is full of the kind of stuff they like: avant garde fashion, the sculpture and handcrafts of friends, Victorian jewelry, and modern camp accoutrements. The thing I admired most was a do-it-yourself psychedelic-light-show kit, containing grids of mirrored glass, a prism, and a mass of colored filters. We started playing with it, catching the sharp, late-afternoon sun through the windows of the shop, and filled the place with cascades of shifting color, spraying each other with showers of purple, green, violet light. It was a great way to end the afternoon, and on the strength of my having bought the light-show kit, Dean and Kim swallowed up their profits by taking me for drinks. Ultimately, they fed me one-third of the lamb roast they had for dinner that night.

In the course of the evening, Dean talked about life in Mendocino. "The town is full of runaways," he said, "or not the town so much, but the hills, the woods. There are communes up there, communal societies trying for tranquillity. And guys who just live in camps by themselves, and come down here sometimes for supplies. It's land's end, you know; there isn't any farther to run, unless you want to jump in the sea. There's even a place up in the hills called 'Lost.' It's for anybody who is. You find it, or it finds you."

Looking up over the gables and white steeples toward the forested hills, I thought how fine a place this was for being lost in. If I ever get lost, and I may, I hope it is there.

running naked at home and abroad

after two years as an Army postal clerk in Germany, I found that I had cultivated a wildly flowering taste for freedom. So it is not surprising that I celebrated my release from the military by taking my clothes off. Even at the time, I dimly realized that I was going to have to perform some profoundly grand and dramatic gesture, to validate my newly allotted independence. Luckily I was in Europe, where the need to be naked in nature is so much more cheerfully accommodated than it is in the States.

Naturally, my dumb show of liberation started with a relatively conservative act of rebellion. On discharge day, April 9, 1959, I did not shave. Instead, I very ceremoniously dropped my razor down the grease trap behind the mess hall. I then marched smartly into the presence of Chief Warrant Officer Joseph A. Pellowski, who stoically handed over my walking papers without commenting on my slightly fuzzy cheeks. I was free—and all the fleshpots of Europe lay before me and my incipient beard.

In fact, it was two beards before which all Europe trembled—mine and that of my old Army buddy Bob Crawford, simultaneously liberated. Between us we had a Volkswagen, five hundred dollars in cash, two well-thumbed and highly suggestive novels from the *Traveler's Companion* series, and the desperate aspiration to get ourselves into as much trouble as possible, just as soon as we could find some. Accordingly, we hastened to put the smoggy, diesel spring of Deutschland well behind us, beetling eagerly down the Autobahn toward the south—to Nice and Cannes and Cagnes-sur-Mer, and all the oily warmth we knew to be there.

It was in the American Express office in Nice that nakedness first came into the picture. I was changing money, and the guy behind the grille asked me if I knew about the Île du Levant. In response to my blank look he at once embarked on a heavily accented encomium: nudist island . . . shared with a naval base . . . bare-breasted beauties waving from the dock at incoming boats . . . a paradise. Crawford and I just about tore up the highway, getting ourselves down the coast to the resort town of Le Lavandou, where launches connect this paradise with the mainland.

In those days, though, the service was pretty spotty, and we had to stay overnight in Lavandou. I remember that we spent the evening drinking wine with a Fulbright scholar's wife who was on the lam and lonely, and that either Crawford or I got awful sick. Whichever way it was, we still managed to make the first boat in the morning, regretfully without the lonely lady, who explained that while she definitely considered herself on the loose, she wasn't *that* loose.

Nobody on the launch that morning looked even remotely loose, unless it was us, red-eyed and hairy. Everybody was sort of settled and middle-aged and respectable, and they took the lurching and wallowing of our small craft with complete equanimity, laughing happily when the salt spray smacked us all in the face. We took it somewhat less well, and after an hour I wasn't feeling terrific. But as the rocky shore of the Île came into view, I felt better at once. There on the dock—could we believe it?—were bare-breasted girls, as advertised, waving at . . . us? No, not so much at us as at our fellow passengers, presumably their aged parents and grandparents, who were even then shucking off their clothes with an alacrity that did credit to their years.

No one was entirely naked, and even the girls on the dock wore the minimum, a tiny triangle of cloth held by a string tied around the hips. But they were all a good bit nakeder than us, decked out in our madras bermudas and white jocksocks and sneakers, like the Ivy League refugees we were. As all the happy families went nudely off on one rocky path or another, we stood stupidly on the dock, wondering what to do next. Finally we chose a rutted road which seemed mainer than the rest, and at the end of a hot and sweaty climb, past all kinds of private villas, hotels, and camp grounds, we came into the center of the village of Héliopolis. It looked just like any little resort village, except that nobody was wearing any clothes to speak of.

Down on the beach, nobody was wearing any clothes at all. I will never forget the shock of my first sight of it. As we came out of a lovely, shady pine grove, to the edge of a cliff hanging over the beach, suddenly there were stark-naked people everywhere. The level of my sophistication in these matters was just about where Thorne Smith had left it in my adolescence, when I purloined from my father's Secret Bottom Drawer Library his novel about some witty people trapped in a nudist camp. Now *I* was trapped in one, and I couldn't think of a single witty thing to say.

However, we had not come this far only to be turned back by something as inconsequential as Total Panic. So, first exchanging a resolute glance, Crawford and I climbed down onto the beach, spread our towels, and . . . took off our clothes. Well, squirmed out of them would be more like it—we hugged the ground and sort of writhed out of our duds, cringing. At once I was overtaken by what American nudists are always calling "the male reflex." Horrors, all I could think to do was to turn my fundament to the sun and my parts to the soil, and pray that my unruly body would get a grip on itself. It was not lust that led to my social predicament; it was pure self-consciousness. But after lying there terrified for about fifteen minutes, hugging the Mediterranean shore with a passion I had brought to few other encounters in my young life, I began to realize that nobody was paying me the least attention, that instead of "exposing" myself in some lewd way, I had actually rendered myself anonymous and unremarkable.

It turned out to be a beautiful day. We wandered around; we met some very nice Swedes and Englishmen and Belgians—families and singles and loving couples—and we swam in the clear, buoyant Mediterranean, than which there is nothing more refreshing, especially without a bathing suit. A French girl with the most stunning superstructure opened sea urchins for me with a scissors, and fed me the edible bits with a tiny silver spoon. And at some point in the afternoon a boatload of voyeurs cruised past, and I waved and hooted at them with the rest.

Later I went walking alone, up into a pine wood beyond the beach. Below me, the blue water was dancing and splashing around the rocks; through the pines, the sky was as blue as the water, cloudless and utterly intense; I was naked in nature, insofar as a man who wears horn-rimmed glasses can ever be said to be naked, and I was loving it. I came that afternoon closer than I had ever dreamed of coming to a transcendental experience, an awareness that I was not only in nature but of it, and I was led to the inescapable conclusion that I could not have had that overwhelming, participatory feeling if I had kept my pants on.

At dusk, we returned to Lavandou. I know now that we should have stayed the night on Levant, but if we had we might never have left. As it was, the Fulbright wife was waiting, and somewhere far ahead, so was all of Spain, and the nameless adventures we were so ready for and could not have done without. Anyway, in an entire day on the Île du Levant not one sexual overture was made or even implied, and we were in a mood for hornier environs.

All that was almost ten years ago. In the meanwhile, I have had my pants off many a time, but never so agreeably as on that first occasion. The sterility of American nudism saps much of the pleasure of running naked at home. Nudist camps in the States on the whole are not free and not much fun, mostly because American nudists are such shocking prudes. Years of institutional paranoia, during which local sheriffs and church wardens had to be constantly assured that nobody was having any fun over at the nudist camp, have led nudists to believe their own publicity. Show me an average group of American nudists and I will show you as dull, not to say as depressingly conventional, a bunch of puritans as you are likely to find outside a Baptist church convention. The only difference is that with Baptists dress is not optional, and that with nudists there will always be some half-wit whose idea of humor is to explode firecrackers and wear lampshades.

I know of only one American nudist club that is an exception to this rule. It has an interesting and varied membership of quite attractive and intelligent people; it has a bar, absolute anathema to conventional nudists; and in October 1968 it made the front page of the *Wall Street Journal* solely because it is a well-run, unhung-up resort for normal human beings who like to run naked. Until recently there were two free beaches on the California coast, just below San Francisco, but one has already been closed and the other reportedly has drawn the fire of local Mrs. Grundys. The deputy sheriff used to patrol that beach naked on horseback, his star affixed to his saddle. The beach was secluded below very high cliffs, it was many miles long, and people could try nudism there without joining or subscribing to anything. When I was there it was a very nice place; I hope it will last but I fear it will not.

The European situation is vaguely similar, but there are many more exceptions. Just as Europeans in general are not so appalled as we are about natural behavior, so European nudists are comparably freer. In Scandinavia there is scarcely any division between nude and nonnude beaches, and nonnudists—that is to say, nudists of the noncard-carrying kind—will take off their clothes quite unselfconsciously on a beach, when they feel like it. In Berlin, where there is a long tradition of indoor nude bathing, there are several saunas and steam baths which are both naked and coed, and they are perfectly chaste and agreeable places. Yugoslavian nudist beaches on the northern Dalmatian coast are still open to anyone who cares to come, but they are quite primitive by American standards. Similarly, the nudist resorts of Corsica were long considered too rough for spoiled Americans, but times are changing. They used to be the sort of places where a Heidelberg undergraduate would spend two years in an absolute state of nature, brooding on Nietzsche and enjoying *Weltschmerz* on a diet of figs. These days, Corsica advertises such sybaritic delights as flush toilets and Tahitian bars, and the trade is picking up. But the welcome is now limited to card-carrying nudists. And all the standard nudist parks in Germany, France, and Britain are closed to adventurous freelancers. There remain only two places on the Continent where anybody can pull his pants off and enjoy an uncommitted taste of social nudism without putting his name to anything more binding than a hotel register—the aforementioned Île du Levant, and the island of Sylt, in the North Sea off the German coast.

For a long time I had wanted to return to Levant, and this summer I decided to make that sentimental journey, and to visit Sylt as well, which I had never seen. I ended by adding yet a third island to my collection—a Scottish one, of all things, at the southern end of Loch Lomond, where you would think people would be freezing to death all the time, what with the low temperature and the fine Scotch mist. But I am happy to be able to report that the Scottish nudists are in good shape, as the Scots tend to be, and enjoy their island just as thoroughly as the French and Germans enjoy theirs. In each case, of course, the style of enjoyment is distinctive and nationally oriented, and you could never mistake one nudist island for another, despite the absence of national dress.

I came to Levant this time under very altered circumstances—I was older by ten years, confirmed in my dislike of the French for their bad manners, not only to tourists but to each other; and sufficiently experienced with nudism that no alarm bells were ringing in my psyche when I arrived at Lavandou for the crossing. Lavandou surprised me; it had been small and unexploited before, but now it is swollen with development, jammed with new white hotels and old brown holiday makers, the side streets filled with gas stations and soft drink stands, the special French sort of tacky commercialism that has made the Côte d'Azur ugly. Motor ferries leave on the half-hour for Levant; they are big, prosperous boats, and they are crowded.

Coming in sight of the island this time, the rocky shore

was not all I saw. The rocks were alive—literally crawling with naked people, like ants scrambling over a smashed nest. The dock was also aswarm with humanity, pushing, shoving, and shouting. A man stood by a beat-up truck bellowing for passengers; very foolishly, I declined to join the cattle drive, and decided to climb up to Héliopolis on foot. An hour later, dragging my suitcases behind me, I was one broken nudist, soggy inside my clothes, exhausted, and still nowhere near Héliopolis. The rattling truck made two trips past me in that time, and I condescended to beg for a ride, but the noisy driver affected not to see me pleading by the roadside.

Finally I reached my hotel—the Brise Marine—reputed to be the best establishment of its kind on Levant. It *was* lovely—a sort of Moroccan and/or Spanish villa, sprawling with courtyards, gurgling with fountains, penetrated by low arched doors. It seemed a fine and secret place for being naked—all the more so when M. le Patrón insisted he had no record of my reservation, and no space available. The island was jammed; I was so parched that I could hardly croak my despair. The patrón relented; for the first night, he said, I could sleep on the balcony over the bar. Perhaps next day, he could find something for me. A Moroccan servant boy was turfed off his pallet above the bar, I was installed, and that was that.

If I had been in any way unprepared for the informality of the Île du Levant, my night in the bar certainly brought me up to the mark. I dozed to the snores of the kitchen help, flaked out by the open hearth, adjoining; by 8 A.M., guests of the hotel were passing through the bar into the dining room, and there I lay, more or less On Display. But it would have been peculiar of me to draw the rumpled sheets about me in embarrassment, considering that the guests were quite as naked as I was, and completely indifferent to what would have been, in any other place, my plight. So I just got up and had breakfast served to me in a sunny courtyard by a grinning, barefooted Moroccan boy, and by my third cup of coffee the world looked somewhat brighter. Somewhat to my surprise, the patrón materialized with a room key, and everybody was suddenly nice to me, and I started to have a good time.

When I was settled in my room and ready to go to the beach, I tied on a minimum which I had had the sense to buy the night before. A gent's minimum is perhaps the world's most obscene garment, which gave me some perverse pleasure in wearing it. To cover a gentleman minimally represents a rather more interesting engineering problem than to cover a lady comparably; the solution is a tiny pouch of cloth, gathered elastically at the back, just big enough to neatly store the masculine equipment. Strings pulled back and tied hold the device more or less in place. Because the island is open to the public, and because it is administered from the mainland community of Hyères, complete nakedness is permissible only on the rocks and beaches and in the hotels or, of course, in private villas. On the streets, the pouch is a necessity. I began rather discreetly with a tweedy beige number, but later I added to my store: a nice blue, with a zippered pocket for cigarettes and odd change; and a flashy Tahitian print in red and white, for festive occasions. It was difficult to choose among them every morning, but it didn't really much matter; as an old college friend of mine used to say, a handsome man looks good in anything.

I stayed on Levant for a full week, and had a thoroughly good time, but I suspect it was because I had friends there, a couple who go every year for at least a month, and they kindly functioned as my social sponsors. Strangers, going in alone without contacts, would be likely to get a very chilly welcome from the regulars, unless they happened to be extraordinarily beautiful of face and figure. A great mind or a brilliant conversational style will get you noplace; a fantastic body and willing ways could lead to anything. In that respect, perhaps, Levant does not differ from any smart coastal resort, except that regulars on Levant are particularly wary of voyeurs and the voyeuristic mentality, and they can spot a leering amateur at once. It does not do to stand around drooling, and it is impossible to stand around drooling, on the beach anyway, with your clothes on. When people come into these areas, as they do every day, fully dressed and voyeuristically inclined, the whole beach erupts with catcalls and, ultimately, physical assault. The cry goes up, *"Voyeur!"* And people point and begin to shout, *"Au poil! Au poil!"* and a good deal worse. You either retreat or get out of your clothes. Last year, when a woman idiotically came onto the beach fully dressed, she was surrounded by naked people making menacing gestures at her and shouting, "To the hair! To the skin!" The poor woman promptly fainted dead away.

This is not to suggest that the Île du Levant is not a sexy place. It is so sexy, in fact, that most regular nudist organizations, in Europe and America, profoundly deplore it. For insiders, Levant is a kingdom of kink, and the restless search for something and/or someone new and different is the basic current of social life. No invitation to lunch or dinner can be taken as simply that, and the most banal conversations are always ripe with innuendo. At the outdoor cafes, where people tend to start the day with *Le Monde* and a pastis; during the long, hot afternoons at the beach, amongst the frolicking children; over dinner by candlelight in hotel dining rooms; at the nightclubs into the very wee hours, the eyes never stop roaming, questing, consulting.

The nightclubs are especially remarkable. The popular spot last year was La Paillote, and it was jammed every night. People usually arrive between ten and eleven, fully dressed as a rule because the evenings are chilly, and carrying little flashlights to guide their way home. La Paillote is like any small, swinging discothèque; the music is deafening, the crush unbelievable, and pretty soon everybody is sweating and drinking and taking his clothes off. Taking his clothes off? Not in New York of course, but in Levant, yes. The ladies usually lead the way, shrugging out of their heavy-knit sweaters, freeing their breasts for comfort. And then the guys, if they are anything like me, are out of their shirts in a flash and asking ladies to dance. It is one of the most agreeable conventions of Levant that ladies rarely refuse a courteous invitation to trip the light fantastic, and by God it *is* fantastic.

Still, it is wrong to assume anything from the looks of things. I remember chatting in a cafe one night with a young Englishman of our group, a Cambridge don named Edward. He remarked balefully that his tent had been empty for several nights.

"What!" I cried. "I thought you were coming on like gangbusters with that German girl on the beach. Doesn't she fill your tent?"

"Well, no," he said. "She seems to want to just beat around the bush."

Jacques, a young Belgian who was with us, misheard the cliché. "I don't understand you, Edward," he said. "You say she wants to beat you in the bushes?"

"Ah, I suppose she would if I asked her," said Edward. "She *is* from Berlin."

I got bored with La Paillote after a few nights—same old faces, same old sweaty bodies—and decided to try another joint down the road. "Oh, don't go there!" a friend said. "*Nobody* goes there this season." But I figured that the entire summer population of Levant could not possibly be crammed nightly into one tiny discothèque, try as they might. There is safety in moving exclusively with one crowd, but I was eager to check out some of the other crowds.

So I went down the road to this other place, which was a little bit quieter than La Paillote, but not much. I got to the bar and ordered un whiskey. The dark girl standing next to me, drinking *her* whiskey, looked me over very frankly and speculatively and then said, "You are English, monsieur?"

"No," said I, somewhat reluctantly. "I'm American."

"Oh," she said, "*Américain*. You look like an English."

Long pause for pulling at our drinks.

She began again. "You are under the impression, perhaps, that the French do not like the *Américains?*"

"Uh . . . yeah, I certainly am."

"There are . . . exceptions, monsieur."

On the strength of that hair-raising innuendo, I bought the lady a drink, and before long she was suggesting that we go to a few other clubs, to see her friends. And we club-hopped the evening away, and were in a noisy stand-up bar somewhere when she said, "Where are you living?"

I said that I had just been settled in a little cottage at the Brise Marine. "Oh," she said. "A lovely hotel. I would love to see it again."

"You WOULD!?!" I cried. "Well, wow, come on." I whipped out my pocket flashlight, we exited into the night, and we set off eagerly for my cottage at the Brise Marine.

Right here I should explain a bit about my accommodations. I had a self-contained cottage on the far side of a courtyard. The cottage had a bath and shower and bidet (very rare on Levant) and a double bed and assorted furniture, but it had no toilet. For such needs one had to cross the court to a communal one-holer. And Josette (for that was her name) and I had scarcely entered the cottage before I was seized with a need to visit that facility.

I lit a candle or two (there was no electricity), invited the lady to make herself comfortable, and set off across the court. What I forgot to do was to warn her about the balcony of the cottage. Workmen had been there all that day, removing the railings. There was a six-foot drop down into a lot of bushes. But since Josette hadn't wanted to visit the one-holer, I figured she'd stay put by candlelight until my return.

Hah. On my way back across the court I heard dim cries, but I couldn't make them out. I hastened back to the cottage. Empty! More cries, less dim. "Deeek," it sounded like. "Deeek!" I rushed out and looked down into the murky blackness below, beaming my flashlight into the dark. And there was Josette, thrashing around in the goddamn bushes and laughing like a crazy woman.

"Oh, Deeek," she said, through gulping bursts of laughter. "I wanted to make pee-pee. It was dark, I step out onto the grass, I think. And boom!"

Boom, you betcha. A six-foot drop—old Josette just plummeted through space into a mimosa. I was frantic. "Are you all right?" I cried, as I dropped a chair down the edge of the balcony.

"I am fine," she said, still laughing. "I am gymnast. I know how to fall. I fall directly on my elbow."

She stepped up on the seat of the chair and vaulted in one leap back up to the balcony. She wasn't even breathing hard, and we later verified that there wasn't a scratch on her.

"I like sport," she said. "Always try to invite to your cottage ones who like sport."

Next morning, the workmen came at nine to replace the railing. Josette said she could not possibly leave. "My family is local," she explained. "I know those workmen and they know me and my family. It would be a grand scandal if they saw me coming out of here, and *dressed*."

"Dressed?" I asked.

"Of course, *dressed*. What will people think that I have clothes on in the daytime? That I did not sleep at home, of course. What girl would create such a scandal?"

So we lay abed all morning, while the workmen worked and cursed outside the door. Josette told me all about Scientology, which she was keen on, and tried to get me to "draw the pain" from her right shoulder with the palm of my hand. But my palm just wouldn't function under present conditions.

At noon, when the workmen broke off and left for lunch, Josette sprang out of bed and begged the loan of a beach towel, which she wrapped as a narrow tube around her loins. All her other clothes—dress, shoes, etc.—she jammed into a shopping bag. And then she was off, almost stark-naked, dressed respectably for daytime Levant.

Later in the month I finally made my way to Sylt, which is not so much a nudist island as an island with nudist beaches. The towns on Sylt are hyperrespectable Germanic settlements, heavy with cleanliness and rectitude, almost prissy with *Nordsee* order and neatness. The three-hour train ride from Hamburg, over the rich, pancake-flat plains, is a suitable preparation for the spare, open quality of Sylt. Westerland, the major town, is the end of the line for a run which brings the train, finally, over a long causeway from the mainland, and oddly, there is nothing islandlike about it. Indeed, on the streets of Westerland one has no sense of sea or beach; continuous high dunes separate the city from the beach, and seem to insulate it from any suggestion of holiday making.

After Levant, I found it difficult to warm to Sylt. My hotel was beautiful and elegant, but blocks from the beach. There was no one on the streets in shorts or other beach-wear, and when I bought my way onto the boardwalk (at a price of DM2.50 per day), I found only Teutonic ladies in hand-knitted sweaters and sensible shoes, marching arm in arm in the salt air, to the military tunes emanating from the bandshell. The entire beach, as far as I could see in either direction, was lined with wicker bath chairs, each one large enough to contain an entire family, set out with Prussian precision and numbered prominently from one to infinity. And everybody in sight was dressed; indeed, the practice is to set out from your hotel in complete costume, strip to your bathing suit within your bath chair, and dress fully again before re-entering the streets of Westerland. Some nudist island, I thought, and repaired to my hotel bar to take something for the chill.

The bartender set me straight; the beach I'd seen was virtually the only nonnudist one on the island. In either direction beyond Westerland stretch miles of open sandy beaches and dunes, and the entire terrain is free, to dress or not to dress. It is because of these beaches, or more especially because of the dunes behind them, that Sylt constantly provides flammable material for the West German scandal sheets. Some fat industrialist is always committing suicide these days on account of what he was seen doing in a sand dune, or photographed in the act of doing, and luminaries have to keep their pants on all the time lest they be photographed bare-ass by the German *paparazzi. Twen* magazine this summer had a big feature which asked the question, *Is Sylt Sexy?* and carried a layout of photographs showing a naked couple cozying up to each other on the back of a Lippizaner grey. To catch a bit of this action, however, I had to go far afield from Westerland, to the duny wastes of Kampen.

In the vicinity of Kampen, the dunes are the thing. There are dunes for every persuasion: wife-swapping dunes, Lesbian dunes, homosexual dunes, troika dunes—you like it, they dune it, and please forgive the pun. By six in the evening, however, the sand is abandoned, and action does not ensue again until about eleven at night, when the small clubs and low joints of Kampen start to heat up. Because these joints have to close at 1 A.M., the well-upholstered crowd rushes up the road to Westerland, where the hours are more commodious. Stand, on any summer evening, at the entrance to a discothèque called the Old Forester, and at 1 A.M. you can hear them coming a long way off—great strings of white Mercedes convertibles, roaring into Westerland with their cargoes of youthful drunks, who spill into the street, snatch at the cap of the doorman, and disappear into the Forester's psychedelic lower depths. The cars stand abandoned any which-way in the roadway.

These people comprise not only an inside set, as in the Île du Levant, but a group impenetrable except via money and influence. The occasional pretty face might be picked up and dropped, for the lark of it, in the course of an evening, but otherwise this is a prohibitive, firmly closed society. However, for casual beach nakedness, in or out of the dunes, all you have to do is walk right or left from Westerland, until the boardwalk gives out, and then walk twice as far, in the wet sand. And abruptly you find yourself in free beach sections, where the wicker bath chair may well contain a lady whose pleasure in sun and surf is unhampered by costume. If you hesitate to rent a bath chair, you can always requisition one of the many deep sand bunkers —great moonscape craters dug everywhere for protection from the wind—pull off your pants and commence to stroll the beach. The surf is rather cold and wicked, and the sun is a sometime thing—the color on Sylt is usually more pearly-grey than golden—but you stand the chance of meeting the most interesting people, and the goose pimples, at least, will be real.

Now let us leave the world of nudism for a moment, though that was not my intent originally, and talk about Scotland. I had heard tell of a nudist island in Loch Lomond, and I thought it would be a great kick to sample nudism on that kind of island after all the sweaty, hot places I'd been checking out. Sure enough, Jim Young of the Scottish Outdoor Club promised me a warm welcome if I came up there, and when I got to London I made it my business to fly to Glasgow and undertake to drive to Loch Lomond. Now I haven't done a lot of touring in Scotland. Would you believe that there were freelance pipers walking the waiting line for the Renfrew ferry? I was charmed out of my mind, though they weren't terribly good pipers. It didn't matter much; the countryside was all a fantasy out of *Brigadoon,* the people of whom I asked directions were extraordinarily kind and nice to me, and the steady drizzle got to seem a bonus.

I was bound for Balmaha, where a ferry leaves twice daily for Inchmurrin, the nudist island—but by the time I was halfway up from Glasgow I knew I'd missed the last boat. So I faced facts, drove round the other end of the loch, and came in quick order to Arden, where I spotted the gates to the Lomond Castle Hotel, and drove right into the tail end of a wedding reception. "Goodbye, goodbye," they were all shrieking as I arrived, and the bride and groom made their getaway down the drive.

The Lomond Castle, a private house until seven years

ago, is one of those hotels run as a private home, and you are a family member except that you don't lift a finger. The crisp, attractive girl at the desk was happy to announce that I could look straight out from the hotel grounds, across the loch toward the island I'd come to visit. She was sorry I'd missed the ferry, but after all there'd be two more tomorrow, or Dick could row me from the boathouse, and meanwhile I might as well content myself with the pleasures of the house.

Lomond is a great, vulgar, nineteenth-century sort of castle, a manifestation of the Industrial Revolution. Somebody made a lot of money, and built himself a castle out of *Ivanhoe,* and it sits today in a green park on the shores of the loch. In the garden, I came on a weathered wooden bench bearing the following verse:

> *The kiss of the sun for pardon*
> *The song of the birds for mirth*
> *One is nearer God's heart in a garden*
> *Than anywhere else on earth.*

Looking around me, I did truly believe it. The park swept away down green slopes from the stern, turreted castle. On one side was a huge, brick-walled garden, the wall falling down in places and screened with apple trees, pruned to the shape and density of ten-branched candlesticks, with bunches of red apples for flame. Inside was a greenhouse of Victorian white wrought-iron drolleries, and there were arbored paths, and Alice's own garden of massed blossom. Along the exterior verge, banked herbs and hollyhocks and every other blooming thing softened the brick, and all over the lawn were circular displays of icy yellow flowers set in sprays of blue-green leaves. Birds chirped, rabbits gamboled nervously from hedge to hedge, and distinctly I could hear the lapping of the loch's tiny waves upon the stony shore.

The kitchen garden was even more appealing: a crumbling gardener's cottage, full of rusty tools, cabbages all in a row, and piles of onions steeping in the sun under glass, intoxicatingly fragrant. At dinner that night, the fresh taste of home-grown foods was the nicest feature of the meal, and as I dined daintily on the tiniest, tenderest sprouts I've ever seen or tasted, I gazed dreamily out on the loch and Inchmurrin, and thanked my Scottish stars that I had missed my ferry, and was here instead of there.

Next morning, I made my way to Balmaha, met Jim Young and his wife at the pier, and boarded a well-polished old boat called the *Margaret* for the trip to Inchmurrin. It was a soggy, rainy day, and Jim deplored the bad weather, but I loved every moment of the voyage out, with the big raindrops pelting down into the grey loch, and the fog obscuring all but the hulking shape of the shore. After about forty-five minutes of our pocketa-pocketa journey across the water, we came to the rickety pier that marks the nudist landing, and leaped from boat to pier when the swell seemed best.

"Ach, can't you smell the bracken," said Jim's wife, as we made our way up a leafy path toward the central clubhouse. "Smoke's rising," said Jim, studying the chimney. "Somebody's here."

We burst into the little house, wet through, to find three or four nudist families fully dressed in their woolies and huddled round the log fire, drinking cups of tea. At once a motherly soul was at me, helping me out of my coat and saying, "Ach, such a day, now let me get you a nice cup of tea." In the whole folksy crowd there wasn't so much as an elbow showing, and I told Jim that I thought the chances of running naked that day were pretty slim.

"Now that's a fact, Dick," he said, "but soon enough I'll take you for a walk as far as the stile, and show you the lay of things anyway." We took that walk, in Wellington boots and borrowed mackintoshes, but Jim didn't leave me at the stile. "I'll walk a wee way with you," he said, and we passed out of the camp grounds and onto neutral ground, where shaggy Highland cattle gazed menacingly at us but forbore to attack. We sloshed through the wet grass, over the high backbone of the island, to a nonnudist boatel, where we got ourselves around a nice glass of beer while Jim swapped stories, unintelligibly, with the local boatmen. Then we sloshed back, where fresh bread, meat loaf, and a cream cake were waiting, and we ate up a storm while the rain hammered on the wooden roof. "Oh, Jim," I said, "I'd like to take my clothes off and run in the rain, and have a quick swim in the loch." Jim and his wife looked at me as if I were touched in the head. "Really, Dick," Jim said, "you'd catch your death of cold. Better bide here with us, and content yourself." So I never got to run naked on a nudist island in Loch Lomond, and I bitterly regret it. Which obviously goes to prove that I am crazier than a Scottish nudist—and me not even card-carrying—yet. It also goes to prove what a good stiff dose of Army discipline can ultimately do for a boy. Loch Lomond is bound to have a sunny day sometime —and I fully expect to be there.

the theater of involvement

there is something fresh and healthy and scary happening in the American theater. It is dangerous; revolutionary. The critics don't like it, but I like it. So take this as a warning of personal bias. I think it is time for this theater in this country, and I am in a stone-throwing mood.

"The language began to effect my cure. For if someone gives me a word for what I'm feeling, the feeling becomes legitimate. It bears a passport; it can freely come and go."

ALBERT GOLDMAN

I am only recently aware that I have been unaware. I didn't know I needed to name feelings before I could have them. As the world's great secret sensualist, I am angry to find that I have been dead to feeling. I am fed up with translating my feelings into intellectual theory, a distilling process which accomplishes total evaporation. So I welcome a kind of theater that jars my unawareness, that tries to force me to be present. Most of us don't like that. We are just not prepared to deal with a theater that doesn't play by the rules, a theater that refuses to be nice. This theater hungers to wrench us out of our secret hiding places, pull us down out of our heads, tear us away from the labels and boxes we call our private lives. This theater wants us to feel.

Scary, no? Violent? You betcha. And let's not, for our own safety's sake, feel anything. Because if we did, boy, how could things go on as they are? And we love things the way they are. Don't we? Now it's not really to worry, because in the first place you don't have to pay money to investigate this troublesome theater. And if you do go slumming for a laugh, "they" can't make you take it seriously, can't really reach you, unless you want them to. You just float off Broadway in your usual perma-sealed polyethylene bag, the same costume that's so comfortable on Broadway, and everything will remain stunningly, divinely impersonal. That is the divine thing, isn't it—God not being dead, really, but just not wanting to get involved.

So I don't think this theater is going to accomplish any "new rebirth of wonder." You can't throttle people into being present, or shock them into anything more profound than the nearest exit. But while you're at it you can bring more excitement and electricity, more fun and frolic and general celebration into our theaters than we have seen ever. The liveliest shows in New York are all outgrowths of the guerrilla theater I've been talking about: *Hair,* breaking all Broadway's rules, and bidding for its records as well; *Tom Paine, Futz, The Concept,* small productions off Broadway; and *Dionysus in 69,* the best of the bunch, an evocation of Euripides' *The Bacchae,* played way downtown in a place called the Performing Garage. All these productions are full of flaws; a couple of them, in fact, are all flaw; but any one of them has more fun in it, and more to do with theater, than anything we have been seeing on Broadway.

For many years the commercial theater has been copping out, busily playing the Establishment game. For season after season, it has failed in all its historic and artistic roles, right down to the final horror, for theater: it has failed to entertain. It has become a theater of sopor and sycophancy, droning congratulatory reassurance at an audience of nodding stockbrokers' wives. Like the careful fool of a medieval court, it has sacrificed its vision for the sake of survival, and the result is that life—the antique transactions of emotion that used to bring meaning to the exercise—has seeped away from the theatrical experience. The American theater is worse than just bad these days; it is boring.

We deserve this kind of theater for being the sort of people we are; having made an indissoluble union between intellect and self, we then added the epoxy of intellectual detachment to secure the union and protect against involvement. So we have a theater that has become a voyeuristic and wholly cerebral exchange, perfectly designed for an audience insulated against experience and unavailable to empathy. It is not our fault, perhaps—but who shall we blame? If we blame our critics, and I would be delighted to, we are really only blaming ourselves, since critics are creatures of our own begetting. And we have begotten a tiny clutch of demigods who, with many an obsequious claim to the contrary, literally design the structure of commercial theater. They are gods of astonishing detachment, immobile on Olympus as Zeus never was, watching and judging from a safe distance which might be called the Gulf of Intellect —that same sea we like to keep between ourselves and the stage. Our critics, speculating and deploring from their Apollonian redoubt, tutor us in how to come to theater. We may laugh and weep for what the players are playing, but it had better be mostly in our heads, for our response must be essentially intellectual. We keep our seats and refrain from throwing things. We have learned to like to keep our cool.

Sometimes press agents find ways to warm up the Broadway igloo. During the unpromising run of *Look Back in Anger,* producer David Merrick secretly hired a woman to climb up onto the stage during a performance and slap the lead actor silly. It hit the papers, of course, and the notion that anybody had been sufficiently moved in a theater to *do* something was titillation enough to sell a few more tickets. What a headline: Scarsdale Matron Angered in Theater. My God, somebody felt something. We better buy tickets.

But I hate to wait for David Merrick to think up something else. And these days, I doubt that a slap would do it. For our intellectual conspiracy against feeling has enjoyed a gathering reinforcement from television. Nowadays, drenched in a bath of electronic waves which wash away all distinctions between fiction and fact, we find all pain play, all play painless. We exist in a time when each of us is the single patron at a multimedia total happening, experience unreeling on all sides in endless bands of celluloid, bearing images of wax bullets, plastic people, and automatic laughter from afar. In this condition of lonely but impregnable detachment, we have wiped out possibilities for personal experience, because nobody is really present at any event. There are not even any real events.

When a man rushes into the street firing an automatic rifle, people rush their children up into firing range so the kiddies can get a closer look. This is not an event; it's entertainment. After the celebrated death of Kitty Genovese, when thirty-seven of her neighbors had watched her murder without calling the police, editorialists deplored the "fear" that kept them from saving the girl's life. The editorialists got it wrong—Kitty's neighbors weren't afraid, they were being entertained. After all, you don't get a murder on your front lawn every day. Who is going to turn off a terrific show like that?

I believe there used to be a time when people felt something—or maybe it was just me. I remember being shown, at the age of fifteen, Actual, Uncensored, Technicolor films of our invasions of Saipan, Guam, and Iwo Jima. It was a treat laid on by an Army colonel, the father of a friend. There was no sound, but we could hear the silent screams we saw. We could understand the agony. And afterward my friend and I, smoking illegally in his bedroom after lights out, said boy, if everybody could see those films, there wouldn't be any more wars. But we were only fifteen at the time, and we didn't know how few silent screams you need to see before you stop hearing them.

Years later, when I was a police reporter in Chicago, I experienced the fact that if you look at enough "dead ones," as the cops called stiffs, if you smell enough blood, you don't really mind it after a while. It starts as reasonable detachment, something you need in order to get the job done. And before you know it, you're a ghoul, and no amount of human suffering, and no measure of joy, can touch you. It is not surprising that under the general bombardment the same thing has happened to a whole people—that is to say, us—so that today we are ghouls too—polite, clean, well-dressed ghouls, courtesy of CBS.

Where was our theater while this was happening to us? It was indulging in isolated grotesqueries, or telling us how wonderful we are, working with the growing numbness as if it were our natural condition, the matter out of which theater is made. Our poets have been shouting the bad news at us for years, but naturally we do not listen to our poets. We do, however, occasionally stumble into Broadway theaters, where our playwrights and our players might have shown us to ourselves. Instead, they hummed our favorite lullabies, and patted us gently all over our spongy, tumescent egos. Curiously, we don't feel the better for it.

It is a strange fact that unless we are thorough fascists about our art, we do not want or expect it to be safe, predictable terrain for us; we do hope it will bring us something we can't get for ourselves: a perspective on the human condition. But when painting and sculpture and music and finally even theater enter avenues of strictly private abstraction, when the arts post notices marked either Something for Everybody or Aficionados Only, when our estrangement from ourselves is pretty well total, we forget that there was ever anything but loneliness. And if we are nothing else, we are adaptable.

So we have adapted to emptiness, and we make Neil Simon comedies do, as if they meant something, somehow. Or a bright playwright writes something very literate, and we dig it for its values as an addition to the literature of the stage, as if the stage were something that originated in a bindery. And occasionally somebody overproduces something really rather small, like *Marat/Sade,* and because we are scared to death by it, we think we are involved. I know *I* was involved in *Marat/Sade*—the wild-eyed actors, in their acceptance of their madhouse roles, persuaded me to accept their psychosis; and otherwise I was personally involved, by virtue of sitting in the second row, to the extent that musicians in the box above my head drooled on my sleeve. When I complained to a member of the cast, he said, "Those damned musicians—always overacting."

But a funny thing happened when I was in London a couple of seasons ago, and saw Peter Brook's production of *US,* an evening of agonizing over the Vietnamese war, an evening in which the cast, from a stance of insufferable moral superiority, demanded of the audience why they didn't feel anything about the war. Toward the end, an actor opened a box and let several butterflies flutter out of it and up into the wings, and we all, actors and audience, watched them fly. And then the actor seized another butterfly, and struck a match, and incinerated the tiny insect while it struggled. And the cast then started to look at us, the audience, and all they did was look, not moving, not saying anything more. No curtains dropped, no lights went up or down—all we had was a cremated butterfly and these actors staring at us. And some people started to applaud and it petered out in the confusion. I thought, Dammit, *we* didn't burn the goddamn butterfly, *they* did. A lot of people then, awkwardly, left the theater muttering, but about half the audience stayed, staring back at the staring players. It was a staring match, until some guy in the orchestra struck back, saying, "I didn't do it. I didn't burn the Vietnamese and I didn't burn that butterfly. *You* did that." He spoke directly to Glenda Jackson, the most obnoxiously effective starer on the stage. "Do you have to sit there like that, or can you talk?" And by God, the evening ended with a big debate, and lots of individual claims to innocence from the audience, and we were yammering in there until the ushers finally put everybody out. Later, Glenda Jackson told me that these debates had evolved only a couple of times before in the course of the run, and no real system had been designed to handle it—least of all, among the ushers.

Not until a press conference which followed a preview of the Broadway opening of *Hair* did I see anything like it in a theater. On this occasion, the cast of *Hair* had done their hair-raising thing for a primed audience, many of whom stayed behind to engage in some sort of dialogue with the director, Tom O'Horgan, and his cast. It had been a wonderful evening of theater—whatever that means. In the course of it, all the mindless attitudes owned and cherished by the American middle class had been rounded up, ridiculed, and disposed of in a delightfully exuberant production. I felt that I had been somewhere, and seen something, and I was grateful for it. But when O'Horgan and the performers came out on the stage and sat down, and questions from the press were solicited, the mood became quickly as mad as *Marat/Sade* and as hostile as *US*. The questions *were* weird: Do you really think anybody is going to stand for a male frontal nude on Broadway? What are you trying to say, anyway? We couldn't hear in the balcony. The response from the stage was condemnatory, despising, bitter. The nasty mood, the "them and us" brutality of the encounter, brought a palpability to the exchange across the proscenium that had not been present during the performance. It was so palpable, in fact, that I had to leave in the middle, because I couldn't take it any more.

It also seemed to me to be wildly beside the point. It was already clear to any but the wholly insensate that *Hair* was a great show by any reasonably viable standards; that it was funny and kinetic and outrageous; that it would be popular. But certain members of the press audience were seizing this last opportunity to voice conventional reservations which the production had already clearly repudiated; and to the authors, to O'Horgan and the cast, this babble of Babbitry from beyond the footlights must have seemed to be the giant Last Straw. Many of them had been working with O'Horgan for the past five years at the Café La Mama, a much-harassed, frequently shifting locale in lower Manhattan where an extraordinary number of young and untried playwrights have had their works produced. Ellen Stewart, who has held La Mama together for many years, struggling against quite unequal odds, sat on stage next to the steaming O'Horgan. She just smiled a Madonna smile —the smile, perhaps, of half a hundred more bitter fights. It may be that she sensed what the others did not, that they had been an underground theater for a long time, and that coming aboveground calls for certain patient adjustments to the glare.

O'Horgan is the focus of all eyes, the Mike Nichols of his day. In addition to *Hair,* two plays directed by him are current off Broadway—*Tom Paine* and *Futz*—both plays, and O'Horgan as well, have been draped in theater awards of an Establishment nature. O'Horgan spent the summer working and lecturing at Brandeis with the La Mama Troupe; alternate casts played *Tom Paine* and *Futz* in sweaty New York. *Tom Paine* was the first O'Horgan production I saw after *Hair,* and it was a strange trip for me, for purely personal reasons. It is playing at a theater called Stage 73, on Manhattan's Upper East Side. After taking a taxi up Third Avenue to Seventy-third Street, my wife and I found ourselves back in our Old Neighborhood, the site of our first apartment in New York. Seven years ago it was a dowdy area beginning to grow spiffy. Now it is unrecognizable. High-rises have replaced the old brownstones, and Stage 73 turned out to be what we had known as Bohemian Hall, a barny old clubhouse for displaced Bohemians. In the old days, we had wandered down to the Bohemian Hall for a glass of Pilsner and a blue-plate special of ethnic eats, and it was all valid Mittel-Europa, down to the gravy stains on the waiter's apron. Now it is mini-mod and plastic Victorian and subdued as to lighting, and too devoted to booze to sell us a couple of cups of coffee before the play began in the theater at the rear. So we went down to the corner of Second Avenue, to a new joint called Graffiti, where they sold us coffee at seventy-five cents a cup in yet another neo-Victorian ambiance, and we passed the time reading the graffiti scrawled on blackboards specially provided for that purpose: BLADDER POWER; CRAIG CLAIBORNE EATS CATSUP; STOKELY CARMICHAEL EATS WATERMELON. It was all a pretty good beginning for our evening at the theater.

The first thing to notice about *Tom Paine* (and it becomes more and more recognizable and admirable as you watch the work of this kind of theater) is that the ensemble is fantastically well disciplined. To create a sense that the stage has been utterly blown apart requires the most exacting sort of stagecraft. That fact, together with the vigor and enthusiasm of the ensemble, were familiar to me from *Hair*. Paul Foster's play makes the argument that Tom Paine was a man, that his time was real, that his faults were human and his life wretched, and that all of this has pertinence to us. To convey that, O'Horgan involves the actors in surreal movement, building vignettes as if he were creating cinematic montage.

Again, the techniques are familiar from *Hair*. But the play does not literally reach out until the action abruptly stops in the middle of the first act, the players pass out cigarettes and incense sticks to the audience, meanwhile attempting to divest themselves of their stage personae, and then undertake to get the audience to discuss the play, to discuss revolution, to discuss specific events outside the theater—riot, rebellion, the mood of national danger. There is no predicting the results of this from night to night, though the ensemble takes the precaution of planting some members at the back of the theater, to simulate argument if none is genuinely forthcoming. But the night we were there, there was plenty of spontaneous backtalk. I would have got into it myself if I were (1) less self-conscious and

(2) more clear about who I was talking to. By that I mean that I could not convince myself that the actors had abandoned their stage presence. I find I cannot argue (except in my head) with written and directed roles. Of course, one of O'Horgan's efforts is to allow the ensemble to work on all the levels of consciousness that obtain at a given time: the actor as himself; the actor as an actor; the actor in the role—the combinations are nightmarish in their complexity. But the problems are all mine. And as I squirmed in my seat, I became aware of all the other squirmers, their bodies advertising their inability to enter the "play" or their certain unwillingness to. During this episode, and through the remainder of the play, my wife and I were intensely aware of the presence of our next-door neighbor in the audience— a tall, stringy young man in a seersucker suit who was participating in his and Tom Paine's anguish with more body English than I was using. When the play was over, we walked down at least ten blocks of Second Avenue and the young man walked "with" us. We would pause, he would linger, we were all intensely conscious of each other and our mutual need to say something—but we never broke through. All we had, when my wife and I finally turned off Second Avenue, was the awareness that we should have and were sorry we had not. And that is, at least, a start.

Futz is something else again; it seems to seek not involvement but revulsion, though perhaps revulsion is a kind of involvement. It is a play by Rochelle Owens, a heretofore unproduced playwright off Broadway, about a man's carnal and sentimental love for his pig. Beyond farmer Futz, the hero and victim of this tragedy, the only gentle and attractive character in the play is Amanda, the pig, and she does not appear on stage. What appears is a collection of vicious hillbillies, mountain trolls, who learn of Futz's cohabitation with his pig and engage in a documentary destruction of the lovers in a mounting frenzy of orgiastic cannibalism. Nothing is solicited from the audience but their disgust, and every conceivable effort is made to win it. Again, the ensemble work is superbly choreographed; you know you are witnessing a hell of a well-wrapped package—and little though I liked it, my distaste had nothing to do with Futz and his pig, whose relationship seemed charming, agreeable, and appropriate. But the attack is off center, built on a play of no discernible merit, celebrating the skills of the players within materials unworthy of their efforts.

Inexplicably, *Futz* has won the "best play" Obie from the *Village Voice*, and a clutch of other awards as well. Yet it is a cold, bloodless exercise compared to *Tom Paine*, and both efforts resemble clinical experiments under glass when compared to *Dionysus in 69*, the most successful attempt at total theater thus far. *Dionysus in 69*, described in the program as "somewhat like Euripides' *The Bacchae*," is the child of Richard Schechner, long-time editor of the *Tulane Drama Review* (now, since Schechner's move to New York, known as *The Drama Review*). A year ago Schechner began forming the Performance Group, a small ensemble of players some of whom had never acted before *Dionysus* evolved as the group's first production. Schechner calls what they are doing "environmental theater," and I have refrained from using that phrase in reference to O'Horgan's work because only with *Dionysus* does it fairly apply. *Dionysus* provided me with the only really complete theatrical experience I've ever had, and in its wraparound intensity suggests undreamed-of possibilities for a viable, live theater in the future.

Dan Sullivan, reviewing the play for the *New York Times,* ended by saying that "anyone who wants to know where the modern theater is going will have to see it." But other critics, notably Walter Kerr, got down to the Performing Garage, Schechner's base way downtown in a dead area of darkened warehouses, and they went all to pieces. Naked bodies, you see, and you have to sit on the floor, and you may be asked to dance, and what Walter Kerr wanted most was a cigarette, and/or out. Sullivan suggested that the evening provides "as faithful a production as *The Bacchae* can have received since its original performance." Too many other critics, caught off base by an environment of total unpredictability, in which the audience is alternately lured and bullied into visceral engagement with the play and the players, gave horrified little shudders and thought it was all too nasty and physical. One critic, his personal hangups displayed in disarray all over his commentary, called Schechner a hoodlum. I have never met Schechner. Third persons have suggested that he is not a very likable man; but the critic in question is himself about as likable as a puff adder, and a deliberately destructive voice in the theater. Whatever else may be said of Schechner, his techniques have breathed life and hope into a moribund art.

When I told a friend of mine, who often writes about the theater, that I was going downtown to see *Dionysus in 69,* he gave the common response. He hadn't been, he wasn't going, and he did a little dance of unease as he said, "I hear they make you *do* things."

"Well," says I, "it all comes with the price of the ticket."

"Oh, no," he said, "all I want for my ticket is the right to watch. Period." Thank you, Walter Kerr and others.

I guess I came to *Dionysus* at a very apt moment, fresh from a visit to Esalen on the Big Sur in California. I wasn't in the Performing Garage very long before I recognized that the players were working with similar kinds of experience. Their absorption and their concentration on a variety of levels of being were familiar to me. And so were the dramatic materials. In college, I had had the good fortune to study Greek drama with William Arrowsmith, long before his translation of *The Bacchae* was published. We worked with it from mimeographed copies he handed out— and here it was again, but really in use—the freshest, most contemporary translation in English. I don't suppose there is any play, Greek or otherwise, that I know better, or studied in more expert company, than *The Bacchae*. But Schechner's interpretation brought the play clear to me at last. Of course, it is impossible to say what Euripides originally intended, and certainly this production is far from anything Euripides would recognize. But the point is that we, the modern audience, *can* recognize it, perhaps with an immediacy similar to its impact when first performed. God knows no other approach to these ancient materials has come so close.

The production grew out of the most intense collaboration among the players, as they sought ways to free themselves for unself-conscious work within the text, examining possibilities and alternatives, allowing their own personalities and personal interactions to shape results. As a consequence, the Dionysus of this play is a young actor named

William Finley, and he's not kidding. He is the god, and he tells us so with overwhelming politesse as he rises, naked except for a black jockstrap, from an intricate knot of similarly naked bodies. "I'm here for three very important reasons," he says. "The first is to establish my divinity." (Guffaws from the audience.) "The second is to establish my rites and rituals." (Puzzled silence.) "And the third is to be born—if you'll excuse me." He then is born, symbolically, through the legs and over the buttocks of the ensemble. "Now those of you who really believed what I said about being a god, about being Dionysus, are going to have a groovy time tonight," he explains subsequently, "but those of you who didn't believe me . . . well, you're in for a bad time of it." I have never seen the point better made that William Finley is as good a name for God as any other, and that the dark and uncontrollable events of the play are universal, born out of the dark and uncontrollable needs and drives of man. I could go on, to linger like the critics over the threatening (or delightful, depending on how you look at it) sensuality of subsequent events. But that would be, as the critics proved by doing it, silly. In a production of extraordinary sensitivity and intelligence, all the critics could see was sex.

Their impacted response is particularly odd in light of the fact that the Performance Group introduces us to a wholly new kind of actor, an actor with deeply involved responsibilities within the ensemble and the play, acting within a creative commune which may call on him to contribute lines of his own dialogue, reinforce the security of his fellow players, strip his body, cope with questions from the audience, and in any and every instant be fully present and answerable for whatever may happen. This is a kind of "acting" which no barnstorming vaudevillian or great profile could even begin to comprehend. This is an actor who can exist only within a deeply dedicated community.

One play, current off Broadway, owes its existence to a community whose central aim is not theater but rehabilitation. It is called *The Concept,* and it is an outgrowth of the work of Daytop, a halfway house for former heroin addicts. As the program explains: "The group met daily for a period of four months in workshop rehearsals. The play evolved as a total group effort through constant discussion and sharing of ideas. Each scene was improvised and worked upon. The improvisations were tape-recorded, and a script was finally created. The play is thus the product of the director and the actors working together in community."

At *The Concept,* the players are ex-junkies, playing themselves. After a symbolic exposition of what life was like before Daytop, the players dig into the kinds of techniques they use to tear down the personal fictions that serve their addiction; they talk their way through the struggles each of them has made toward commitment, trust, and love. The cast is very good, and it is difficult to remember that these bright, attractive people are not actors pretending to be in trouble, but bright, attractive people who are in trouble. Toward the end of the play, during a marathon encounter, one of the girls is asked if she thinks anybody loves her just for herself. "Just for myself?" she asks. She first argues that she's sure of everybody's love, but it turns out that there is one person in the room whose love she doubts, and she is encouraged to ask him if he loves her. After a terrible struggle she is able to ask the question. The answer

is yes, of course, and she knows it; the agony of the moment
is not in the answer but in the terror of the question. "Will
you love me?" she asks, and he says yes, and they embrace
and then sit quietly together, past uncertainty into peace.
The confrontation is repeated one more time, with two of
the men. And then these people get up and, smiling gently,
go out into the audience and ask various people, directly,
"Will you love me?"

It was a searing moment in my theater experience; it
hurt in my throat. One woman, asked to love, burst into big
boo-hoos. But I heard one guy leave the theater singing sar-
donically, "Will you love me in September as you did in
May?" There is no telling, in advance, how you will react
to the theater of involvement. You have to go to the
theater, and see.

my god! they're naked!

i know a girl who, until she was seventeen years old, always dressed and undressed in the closet. With the door shut. With the light off. Because otherwise she might catch a glimpse of herself, see. It was something she learned from her mother.

I mention this because the subject is nudity in the theater —or would it be all right to say nakedness, which appears to be the less acceptable term? It seems that nudity implies artful undress, while naked means stripped, which is somehow more ghastly. Anyway, in either term, there is a lot of it these days in the theater, and I like it—often for quite unelevated reasons, of course—but the point is that certain elements of the theater are well ahead of us in the body business. There is a new maturity abroad about bodies— not just in the theater, but highly noticeable there, quite rightly—and society is still dragging its heavy leather heels. For example, it is now about twelve years since that girl whispered her terrible secret to me—as I recall, it was a party weekend at Vassar (Mary McCarthy take note)—and while she may be an extreme case, we are still doing this kind of closet thing to children, giving them hangups they don't need and we're not over, hangups we persist in as if we had to.

Meanwhile, a sort of theater is emerging that tries to deal frankly and honestly with the human body—not only as an instrument of the drama but as the whole persona of each actor, a complete organism from tip to toe, which he learns to accept and use with extraordinary freedom.

This is a great breakthrough for the actor, for the theater, and hopefully for society—though the last depends on whether audiences can be available for the kind of awareness that the actor is working with. And because, through generations of instruction and habit, we have learned not to accept our bodies, we tend to have a tough time accepting the actor's acceptance, much less the fact of his body, naked (perhaps) before our eyes. The hangup, I hasten to say, is not his but ours—we are habituated to something very different in the theater.

What we know and love in this line is the antique bump-and-grind school of peekaboo flesh—we feel safe with it because we grew up with it, accepting its limitations in a friendly spirit of fraud. This we like. And if we can turn on this way to sequined nipples, it must have something to do with how we regard ourselves, and how much our bodies are us. It is my observation, available to dispute, that we tend to live fairly exclusively in our heads, peering out from our eyes as if they were the conning towers of our control center. The rest of us we drag along as sort of attached ganglia, awkward, embarrassing, often painful, but dammit, there. We wash this body, and cover it—and perhaps, in moderation, occasionally we make it available to localized titillation. But we aren't really *in* it.

So then a noisy, bumptious musical called *Hair* comes to Broadway, and at the end of the first act, every night, those cast members *who want* to take off their clothes, stand up, and face the audience. Naked. There is a point to this: one of the leads is singing a lyric to this effect—Now you see us, see who we are; what are you going to do with us, where are you going to send us? And the boys and girls are standing there mother-naked, saying in effect, This Is My Body, This Is Me. Now the audience, however good-willed, is still all heads attached to ganglia, so what are they going to do? Will they get the point? Probably not, and they will go to the office next day and talk about the crazy skin show they saw. This despite the fact that psychedelic lights are whirling blindingly during the naked scene—a rather specialized sort of copout for which director Tom O'Horgan ought to be ashamed. The point is strong enough—and if you're going to be naked, be naked, not bathed in electronic coveralls.

Anyway, even without special lenses the audience can

just see that the boys and girls are naked, and that they are complete, male and female. In a time when members of the population think that little boy dolls with little boy penises will debauch American children, imagine what the sight of fully developed big boys ought to do to the audience. By contemporary community standards, regularly articulated in our courts and customs houses, that audience should be instantly set on a wild course of bestiality and rapine. Curiously, however, audiences have been behaving with laudable restraint in the face of this provocation, though a few people do walk out of the theater every night. It can't be in *surprise*. Maybe, by going in and walking out, they are making some elaborate ceremonial gesture of contempt for the human body. Their motive eludes me, but this I do know and sadly deplore: if the boys and girls of *Hair* made their statement while strategically covered in pasties and rhinestone jockstraps, their presence on stage would be offensive to almost no one. It would also, of course, be a lie.

It is the lie we like, for it belongs to our long past, to the leering, masturbatory peep shows of the American theatrical tradition. After all, what's an impresario to do? With a public both hysterically uneasy about sex and desperately itchy for it at the same time, what shall he serve? Burlesque, why not, and strip-tease, the G-string ,and the posing strap. On Broadway, we get the deliberately salacious sniggering of the musicals that glorify what they pretend to parody; in *Golden Rainbow,* for instance, the professionally wholesome Steve Lawrence and Eydie Gorme are supposed to offset the gilded nudity of a second-act spectacle that panders to our taste for simulated Babylonian orgies. Our entertainers have, to do them credit, given us what we wanted, which was and still is an evocation of private reverie—in doses from the White Rock girl and September Morn right through the Ziegfeld showgirl to the Sweater Girl, the Body Beautiful, and the Million-dollar Chest. Alas, they are all rattling specters of Boyhood Past, wispy relics of the time when every kid fears he is either a rapist or a madman—thus for our commercial theater, as for us, the human body has yet to advance beyond the standards of an adolescent wet dream.

But we were speaking of honesty. The theater of involvement, from which I draw my better examples, does not always work as honestly as it might in this line. The busy, obscuring lights of *Hair* are one copout; O'Horgan makes another in his production of *Tom Paine*, which includes a celebrated "nude" scene. In this case, in a production commendable in many ways for its efforts to bring a sort of documentary surrealism to the stage, there is a scene in which Paine, languishing in an alcoholic miasma, is about to be assaulted by erotic fantasies. Accordingly, the members of the cast leave the stage, each with, I regret to say, an exit line, and if they each held up a cautionary finger they could not more underline what the audience already knows, that the nude scene is Coming Up. The players rush to the wings, strip off their black leotards, and glue themselves into some sort of blue gauze draperies, securely fastened at shoulder and thigh. In this state of spurious and oddly prurient nudity, they re-emerge to haunt Tom Paine as erotic phantasms, waving their arms and going Woo-Hoo at him, their bodies lurking dark and smoky behind the taut gauze. Now once again, what is this? The scene would have been equally effective if the cast had left on its leotards. For erotic fantasy, Tom O'Horgan should have been able to do better than this, or have left it alone.

One worries about the cashbox, of course, and the cops, who have on their minds something rather approximating Marian purity in dress and demeanor, and who can, by harassment, break a small-money show in short order just by leaning on it. You can't blame the cops; by their lights they find themselves presiding over the Fall of Rome, and it troubles them. So they hang about, ostentatiously, in places where they think it might be a deterrent at the box office. One place they like is 33 Wooster Street in downtown Manhattan—the address of the Performing Garage—where *Dionysus in 69* is performed. Apart from lurking, the police have not interfered with *Dionysus,* possibly because obscenity statutes have shilly-shallied considerably of late. It is just as well—the play is pretty naked, as critics were quick to point out, and that fact alone would have made it unplayable in Manhattan not many years ago. But its nakedness is not its point, though in the remarks of critics one would think so.

The undress of the production is a costuming appropriate not only to the orgiastic nature of Euripides' play but to the gymnastic nature of the production as well. The ladies are always discreetly covered, but the gents work mostly in black-dyed jockstraps, and at least one critic has complained of what he could therefore see. Because in their view *Dionysus* threatens the intellectual pretensions of the theater with its invitation to visceral engagement, some critics have called these people gangsters and hoodlums. These critics admitted to having felt personally, physically threatened by the nudity and nonverbal language of the production. Yet not one member of the ensemble could be accused of pandering in any way to the lewd hangups of anybody, a charge that could be made almost scattershot elsewhere in the theater. This company seeks simply to work with every resource it has, and with as much honesty as it can muster. The effect is total—it reaches beyond the theater into the cast's personal lives and ambitions—and it suggests a new and highly responsible theater for the future. If that is gangsterism, our society is in a very bad way.

Dancers have got away with this for years, this gangsterism—perhaps in part because their work is already accepted as nonverbal, in part also because they belong to a performing art that has long been thought to have little influence beyond the small recital hall. In my time I have heard many a dancer put down as a narcissist because of his or her absorption in nonverbal language, the fact and the movement of the body, in the body as an instrument of communication. Oh, she's very pretty, they say, but stupid. Hasn't anything to say. But the times are moving us toward a synthesis of theater and dance, and more people are realizing that dancers were onto something more than narcissism all this while. While the theater was locked in its head, despising anything nonverbal, the dancers were beginning to celebrate their bodies, to evaluate all movement in terms of artistic validity. Ruth St. Denis and Ted Shawn were exploring physical vitality and its primitive expressions in the 1920's; Martha Graham has been the leading talent of our time; now comes Ann Halprin from San Francisco, into New York with her Dancers' Workshop and a number called *Parades and Changes* that electrified a

Hunter College audience last year because the eight attractive young people took off their clothes and worked with rolls of brown paper. "As naked as berries," Clive Barnes explained, a curious Victorian coda to Ruth St. Denis's statement of many years ago: "The best garb is no garb."

Dancers do usually love their bodies, and have never shown any great reluctance to display them as fully as possible. Ted Shawn, once a student for the ministry, believed in the power of the naked human body to express spiritual values; his great ambition, never realized, was to dance nude on a major American stage. He and the Denishawn dancers, mostly college athletes, worked and lived largely in the nude at Jacob's Pillow, attempting to conjure a sort of "palaestra of ancient Greece" in the Berkshires. Their work in public tended to support Shawn's ideas of Greek ideals, and was, where appropriate, scarcely costumed at all.

The Greek thing has pretty well died out among dancers these days, who no longer seek some rationale of "purity" for dancing naked. Rationales are still sought, however, because the sheer joy in naked movement is not yet a popular or even acceptable concept in our country.

John Graham, a dancer and faculty member at San Francisco State College, was once one of Ann Halprin's principal dancers, but split with her on the question of how the dancer ought to consider his body when nude. "Ann thought we ought to consider the skin as just another costume," he said, "and I couldn't accept that. Skin is not a costume; it's the surface of my body. And if I'm naked, I'm naked." In addition to his teaching at State, Graham is doing very interesting things in dance with his wife, a lovely girl named

Jani Novak, and an old friend and former Halprin dancer, A. A. Leath.

They meet once a week at a small hall in Berkeley, to move to the interior rhythms of their relationships with one another. Any old music is played; the aim is not aesthetics, but an exploration of the emotive powers of the body. The night I was there, in the midst of perhaps a hundred other people, the three dancers moved to a spectrum of emotions— there were anger and jealousy, clearly articulated, but also humor, joy, and a great deal of love. Ultimately, the dancers began to draw spectators onto the floor, to move with them, to move in larger groups, or to move alone as the need was felt. In the end a hundred people were moving happily and completely freely around the floor. Some clothes came off, but not mine; I can be naked in nature but I couldn't manage it in a nightclub. However, I did find myself making wide, arm-flinging gestures and turning cartwheels, as I haven't felt free to do since I was a kid. It was a beautiful evening.

Meanwhile, the Living Theatre, the prototypical ensemble in the movement toward existential, wholly involving theater, has come home from European exile with a new production called *Paradise Now*. Julian Beck and Judith Malina, the ensemble leaders, have already been busted in New Haven for allowing *Paradise* to spill out onto the streets, with its improvising actors and audience in various states of freedom from clothing. Naturally I want to be there when *Paradise* comes my way. The newspapers make no mention of cartwheels, but I'm pretty sure the Living Theatre wouldn't object. And maybe this time I might even get up the nerve to take off my shirt.

living with the living theatre

diann and Nathan and Jean and I have been having martinis and chicken-liver shish-kabob at Nathan's apartment, and now we are on our way to the Brooklyn Academy of Music to see the Living Theatre's *Paradise Now*. We are late, Nathan has never driven to Brooklyn before, and we are not sure of our directions, Brooklyn being most definitely Another Country for all of us.

We zip down Second Avenue, enjoying the plush pizazz of Nathan's fancy black convertible, and I remark that we are already experiencing the Living Theatre, because we are living and on our way to it. As I dimly understand, the Living Theatre's argument is that theater must be life, and life theater—and the fusion is already accomplished by our noticing its possibilities. Everyone praises me for the observation, and I feel clever and smug.

Fairly promptly we are in the maze of lower Manhattan, and I direct Nathan over the wrong bridge. In a matter of minutes we are lost. So we pull into the first gas station we see, where a cop is leaning on the fender of his squad car. Diann rolls down her window and says, "Excuse me," and instantly the cop says, "One block past the Fox Theater and turn left." Diann says, "We didn't say where we were going yet." And with the bored, knowing sneer of the New York cop he says again, "One block past the Fox Theater, left turn."

He takes one look and he *knows* us. It's as if we were wearing badges. Obviously, the Living Theatre is drawing whole bunches of un-Brooklyn-type people into Brooklyn. Diann is certainly un-Brooklyn. She is more like Miss Short Hills, New Jersey, of All Time. What would Miss Short Hills be doing in Brooklyn except to see the Living Theatre? Or indeed, any of us? Yet all we have in common with the Living Theatre is that neither they nor we belong in Brooklyn. We talk about how that is not really much of a bond.

We have seen pictures of the Living Theatre company in the papers. Squatting, in loincloths, in Spoleto. Being thrown out of Avignon. We have read abuse of them, by critics, in all the best papers and magazines. We know they were busted in New Haven, when as a consequence of passions raised by *Paradise Now* at Yale, they and the audience "took the revolution into the streets" without no clothes on. We understand that *Paradise Now* is designed to be an act of anarchy. We want to experience the Living Theatre's brand of anarchy, to know who they are. But we feel we are not *like* them. They are, for one thing, so frighteningly noisy and hairy.

The cop's directions are precise, and we are lickity-split parked alongside the Academy of Music, a building none of us has ever seen before. It is a brilliant imitation of a Viennese concert hall. We enter the all-marble lobby, and under glittering chandeliers pass posters promising us Oistraikh and Isaac Stern, Clifford Curzon and Mstislav Rostropovich To Come. We hurry into the auditorium where an incredible sight confronts us. We are in the most unremarkable, expectable sort of theater space, with orchestra and balcony seats facing a wide proscenium stage. But nothing else is expected. Hundreds of people are milling about on the stage. Many more hundreds are milling about in the aisles and churning forth and back among the orchestra seats. An usher materializes out of the crush and shows us to our seats, about ten rows from the back. On our way there, a wild-eyed girl rushes up to Diann and says, most intimately and urgently, "I don't know how to stop the wars." She then rushes on to say this to someone else. We rush on, in new confusion, to our seats.

We settle in. A long-haired boy leans over between Jean and me and says, with trembling desperation, "I don't know how to stop the wars." I don't either, and I am as troubled about it as he seems to be, and I am at once involved. Everywhere in the auditorium, wild-looking people are saying the same thing, and they are getting more and more desperate and loud. Finally people are running up and down the aisles, shrieking at us, "I DON'T KNOW HOW TO STOP THE WARS." And then they all begin to scream horribly. Then silence. And then a girl comes over to me and says, very quietly and almost secretly, looking deeply into my eyes, "You can't live if you don't have money."

All around us, other people are getting the same message. The whisperers stop everyone to whisper it, then to speak it conversationally, then to shriek it anxiously, finally to scream it at large, "YOU CAN'T LIVE IF YOU DON'T HAVE MONEY!" A boy is shouting this into my face, inches away. While I'm listening to what he is saying, understanding the significance of the words, perhaps for the first time in my life, I realize that it really is horrible that we can't live without money. The boy begins to scream piercingly, doubling over with agony, and everywhere in the theater people start to scream, and it is a universal, enveloping shriek to heaven.

Silence. The unison scream resonates in the sudden quiet. And pretty quick a girl comes up and says to me, in the now familiar, confiding manner, "I'm not allowed to smoke marijuana." The whole pattern resumes, building and growing to the same hideous scream, but suddenly I find myself withdrawing from involvement. I like marijuana, and I am continually annoyed that government and society haven't changed what I feel to be stupid, irrational laws. But it is not a subject so important to me as the fact that we cannot live without money. Without marijuana, we can live.

I next hear somebody saying to me, "I'm not allowed to take my clothes off." Aha—the body taboo—now we're back to something I care about. The frenzy, the anxiety, the anger builds—but this time not to a scream. The members of the company take off their clothes instead, stripping to the most minimal genital covering. Thus identified by their nakedness, they make their way to the stage. Among them we notice Julian Beck, the leader of the company. Not only is his vocal delivery strong and clear, but his appearance is so stridently bizarre that he can't be missed—a tall, emaciated man with the look of a prophet; long hanks of hair descending from the edges of a middle-aged bald spot.

Deftly making space among the pushing throng on the stage, the company does a tableau or two. One seems to represent Indians being shot while on some fanciful warpath, and it is effective. But between tableaux everything seems to descend promptly into chaos. Diann and Nathan decide to walk down toward the stage, and quickly are swallowed up in the mob. Jean declines to leave her numbered seat, but I want to see what's happening, and I leave her. Down under the footlights the crush of people is almost asphyxiating. A group near me is complaining loudly that what is happening is not anarchy but playtime; "This isn't revolution, man," they are saying. "This is bullshit." A pretty girl is red in the face from shouting. "You motherfuckers," she screams. "You do this shit for a bourgeois audience. Why don't you get out on the motherfucking streets and try it?"

Frightful scenes are occurring just by me. A middle-aged, grey-bearded man and his wife are loudly abusing the jammed-in people standing in front of them. "Son of a bitch," says the bearded man. "I paid for these front row seats and we can't see a fucking thing. Get down in front."

Apparently he hasn't noticed yet that there *is* no "front," and that the number on his ticket has nothing whatever to do with where he is allowed to sit or stand. "Did you *pay* for that space?" he demands of a boy in front of him. The boy peers back over his shoulder. "Why don't you cool it, man?" he asks. "This is free theater—if you don't like where you're sitting, go sit someplace else."

The man's wife is outraged. "Did you hear him?" she asks at large. "Punk kid, saying '*man*.' That's kids. That's the younger generation. No respect."

Bearded companions of the pretty, red-faced girl are shouting at one of the naked boys. "Free theater, *bullshit!* If it's so fucking free, give us back our fucking $5.50."

"That's great," says the naked kid. "Tell me more—louder."

At the front edge of the stage a big-bellied girl has thrown herself down on her back. She has mad eyes, and she dandles a tiny baby, about eight months old, on the wide expanse of her stomach. Oh wow, I think, that baby should be at home. Can that crazy girl be the mother? The girl shouts obscenities at the Living Theatre people and at everyone else, shaking her baby for emphasis as if he were a loose towel in her fist. The baby begins to cry, but in the general roaring his thin wail can scarcely be heard. I notice that Julian Beck materializes out of the crush, takes the baby and cradles it gently, while another loinclothed actor begins to speak quietly to the mother.

There is a general surge up onto the stage and I join it. It *is* novel to find myself *on* the stage instead of looking at it. Hundreds of people are up there with me, pushing, shoving, and sweating. Smoking, embracing, taking off their clothes, chatting in small groups. Members of the company clear a circular space in the center of the stage, sit in a circle, and do some sort of hand dance. It is hard to see because we are all sitting down now, pressed up against one another on the floor. People are smoking, and none too careful about crushing out the cigarette stubs. I wince at the thought of all the bare feet that could step on glowing stubs.

Suddenly we are standing and there is a surge of movement off the stage and into the orchestra. I am pushed and pulled along to the edge of the stage, while the man next to me joyously shouts, *"Fire! Fire!"* At the edge of the stage I pause and see Nathan and Diann sitting goggle-eyed in the second row. I don't try to join them—we are at least a fifteen-minute struggle apart. Instead, I fight my way up the aisle to the rear, and find Jean sitting happily where I left her, engaged in amiable dialogue with a naked actor and three or four other spectators.

Someone has given Jean a program, a vast scroll which appears to divide the evening's events into a series of eight "rungs," ascending toward the final taking of the revolution into the streets. It is already ten-thirty and we are not yet very close to the streets. The naked actor explains that each of the rungs is divided into three stages, the first two carefully preplotted, the third dependent on the response of the mob. The entire ascendancy is explained by a program note: "The essential trip is the voyage from the many to the one." Jean stares bleakly at the huge program and asks, "Do you always make the whole trip?" The actor smiles at her warmly. "Always," he says. "Always."

Jean and I fight our way out to the lobby, past people making up free posters in the causes of love and peace. Insanely, there is a man in the lobby selling sticky orange juice and slim mints at Broadway prices. We go outside, we stand on the steps, and we breathe. "God, the air is like a tonic," I say to Jean, while she nods numbly, breathing greedily. We talk about the actors, who have been working and sweating so hard that, when they pass in the aisles, they leave an almost palpable spoor behind. "They smell bad," I admit sadly. "The critics have always mentioned it and I thought they were just being nasty. But you have to face the fact that the Living Theatre stinks."

We struggle back into the auditorium, find fresh seats toward the rear, and let the ensuing action wave and crash about us. Occasionally I try to figure out where we are in the program; we never seem to be very far along. Jean dozes. On the stage, a naked black actor is going into a violent racial statement. "I hate you white sonsabitches," he rages. "You fucking cocksuckers. Since I was fourteen all I ever heard was 'nigguh.' You a very talented nigguh. You got a fine nigguh body and a deep nigguh baritone. (Laughter in the auditorium.) And you wonder why we so mad? Why don't you honkies wake up? Wake up!"

Jean's chin is on her chest. She is sound asleep. "Wake up! Wake up!" The actor shouts it over and over. Jean dozes on. The actor is in a frenzy, pacing back and forth, shouting. He *has* got a fine body, and it is glazed and glistening with sweat, beautiful to see. He seems to be made of moist milk chocolate. I notice that Nathan and Diann are still down front, but now they are standing up on the arms of their seats, talking to some other people. They appear not to be listening to the actor.

I notice that it is midnight. The actors are performing a set piece entitled "The Vision of the Magic Love Zap." A tall, skinny boy at the end of our row is talking to a girl, and I overhear. "Really," he tells her pompously, "there is, in itself, no conceivable value in taking off your clothes *just* to be taking off your clothes." Five, ten, perhaps thirty minutes later, I notice that he has taken off his clothes and is wandering in the right aisle in nothing but his jockey shorts.

At one o'clock Jean revives slightly. The theater is relatively quiet and completely dark while the actors perform an arrival on Mars, and Jean explains that the sudden quiet has startled her awake. We still do not seem very close to the streets, and I stir in my seat in search of Nathan and Diann. I'll never find them in this chaos, I think, but I hear Nathan right behind me, saying, "Looking for us?" They have been there for at least an hour. One by one, we make our difficult way into the lobby. Nathan is the last to arrive. "Well," he says, "this isn't so much theater of involvement as theater of endurance." His shirt is completely unbuttoned but he is buttoning it up. "Julian Beck would not like you to button up your shirt," I say. "I just did it automatically," he says, automatically unbuttoning it again.

We stand around, comparing notes, deciding that even the boredom and fatigue we have been experiencing are necessary to *Paradise Now*. We admit that even negative involvement is involvement, and we are determined to see the goddamn thing through to the end.

Nathan and Jean go back in; Diann and I smoke cigarettes, then follow. Glory be! The revolution is on its way to the streets, actors and audience spilling off the stage and making for the lobby. People are automatically putting their shirts and socks on, all over the theater. Diann remarks that it is not a very revolutionary audience. We sit down to let the throng pass.

Behind us a girl is saying to her escort, "I'm tired. That's all. I'm just tired. I'm tired of people shouting at me."

Her boy friend stares at her, mock-annoyed. "You always bring up your mother," he says.

Laughing, we push back out of the auditorium again, to find that the revolution has not arrived in the streets. Rows of New York cops stand in front of the Academy of Music, stifling nakedness on Atlantic Avenue before it ever gets a toehold.

"Now *that*," says I, "really makes me want to take my clothes off."

"Me too," says Diann.

Short Hills, New Jersey, will never be the same. It appears, however, that Brooklyn will endure.

i am curious (yellow)

ladies and gentlemen, I am pleased to announce, in my official capacity as Dedicated Lifelong Moviegoer of our time, that the world's first honest flick has been made and is alive and well and totally isolated in Stockholm. The world's censors, it seems, are not ready for *I Am Curious (Yellow)* [at least, they weren't in December of 1968, when this piece was published]. The title requires almost as much explanation as the film itself and, because of its imponderability, has occasioned such erroneous locutions as "I Am Curiously Yellow." By whatever misnomer, *I Am Curious* was for a time on the tip of every forked tongue in New York, as a device for turning cocktail conversations toward the subject of sex; the film contains many perfectly straightfoward scenes of sexual intercourse in a variety of *tableaux vivants,* a feature of the production which has given rise to the loose assumption that *I Am Curious* is a dirty movie.

I suppose that persons for whom sex itself is dirty would find scenes of sexual intercourse incorrigibly offensive, wherever they might occur and in whatever context; for me, it was a refreshing and happy experience to see human sexual relationships played straight, with neither licentious giggle nor strategic fade-out, for all the world as if sex were a natural, integral part of human life. For me, it confirmed the integrity of the director and the players, and projected an unexpected aura of wholesome candor. I think it is a squeaky-clean flick and I think the handling of sexual matters is admirable, but most of all I think you should know that not only is it distinctly not a dirty movie, it's not a sexy movie. It's not even *about* sex—any more, say, than it is about war. Or youth and earnestness. Or personal honesty. Or love.

To some, this argument will sound like the most predictable liberal sophistry—yet another fuzzy-minded apologia for Our Rising Crime Rate, the Breakdown of Morality and Riot in the Streets. Sexual congress on the screen at the Orpheum—Holy Gomorrahville! I'm aware of the pitfalls in this advocacy, especially among surface moralizers, but I cannot see that along with *I Am Curious* comes Armageddon. Nor do I care to argue, as others might, that sexual frankness belongs to the Scandinavians the way female circumcision belongs to the Yoruba; that it's okay on its home ground but should not be available for export. There they go again, those silly lubricious Swedes, up to their usual antiseptic, blond bawdry—that attitude doesn't wash either. The Swedes may be a coiled hair or two more accepting of their sexuality than we are, but as a people they are just as phony and frightened of themselves as Americans are—a major point, by the way, of *I Am Curious.*

That point, together with many others, is one the feds missed when they acted to ban the movie from the United States. Picture a typical afternoon over at the customs shed, where we find Mr. Irving Fishman, Commissioner of Customs in New York, tirelessly screening imported foreign flicks, red-eyed and vigilant in the cause of American purity. Suddenly what flickers before Fishman's face but . . . can it be? . . . Are they really? . . . Horrors! One look was all it took—upon which, out went the Lifted Lamp, slam went the Golden Door. Scratch one Swedish movie, courtesy of Irving Fishman.

How then, I hope you'll ask, come I to know so much and talk so fancy about this evil movie Mr. Fishman has taken all this advance trouble to protect me from. Travel, gang—travel is the answer—so broadening, so educational, so sharp a thorn in the federal flesh so very often. Now, to be sure, I didn't fly to Stockholm *solely* to see a notorious movie. Happily, I had other business in Europe, and as long as I was there, I thought I might as well imitate the English, who fly to Stockholm for the weekend to see *I Am Curious.* Sole purpose of visit. I couldn't claim that much single-mindedness; nevertheless, it gave me the most enormous pleasure to get the best of Mr. Fishman, just this once. And I swear if I had a lot of dough I would fly anywhere to thwart his plans for me. U. S. Customs is always behaving like the fat lady in the theater who won't remove her hat. I wish those guys would pay more attention to heroin and poisonous red berries, which presumably they know how to recognize. It is certainly a cinch that they don't know a fine movie when they see one.

Finding *I Am Curious* in Stockholm is like finding out where *Dr. Zhivago* is showing in New York; it's not exactly the hottest new release, and even with careful instructions from the concierge of my hotel I managed to get lost on back streets far from Stockholm's Great White Way. It wasn't stupidity so much as fatigue, after a long night flight with an ugly stewardess, a chilly dawn arrival, and a day of wandering around, reacquainting myself with the lovely, indefinably northern city. I had forgotten what a livable city it is—how clean and how whisper-quiet, even at rush hour; I don't know how they manage it.

As I stumbled along, making one wrong turning after another, I found myself brooding grumpily on the Swedish character. No wonder: I was tired and lost and my cigarettes were beginning to taste like tinfoil—I took it all out on the Swedes. Soullessness, a lack of warmth—a people thought to be too smug, abrupt, and businesslike; the men stiff and formal, the girls, though meltingly lovely to look at, cold of heart, with icy toes. A cold people in a cold country, where thirty years of democratic socialism have meant a fair shake for everybody and rising suicide rates for all, with interim interludes of free sexuality, just to pass the time. I thought of all the silver-haired grannies in all the little tobacco shops, sweetly tending whole walls of pornographic wares. Oh, you don't care for multicolor Lesbianism? Now here's a popular one—and she's handing you a glistening slick magazine with a single, monumental male member, rampant on the cover. Those sweet little old ladies —they absolutely blew my middle-class American mind.

In this unpleasant mood I accosted the next man I saw and almost rudely asked for directions. He was a young student from the look of him, shaggy sweater and Levi's and lots of hair; not only did he know where the movie house was, but he was bound there himself. As we walked along I complimented him on his excellent English, scarcely any accent at all. He thanked me warmly, and revealed that he was Australian.

At the movie house there was no difficulty about tickets and no crush in the lobby, and so far as I could overhear, the audience was almost exclusively English-speaking. When the movie came on with subtitles in English, I was able to feel completely at home. I needed to, because right away I was in trouble trying to follow *I Am Curious*. If I hadn't had those subtitles, I would have been hopelessly lost.

Vilgot Sjoman, the director of *I Am Curious,* has constructed what he calls a kaleidoscope of kinds of awareness; in other terms, it is as if bits and pieces of pictures and print were assembled in a collage. The interdependency of the elements creates a cumulative effect; bust up the elements, and you have only bits and pieces again. But cinematic collage is a tougher form than anything static—more effective, perhaps, once an audience is able to allow the technique to work, but at first, as perplexing as a Chinese box.

This is as good a point as any, I suppose, to attempt to explain the (*Yellow*) of the title. The Swedish flag is yellow and blue; Sjoman has both yellow and blue versions of the same film. What startled me most about *I Am Curious* is that its central subject, as "yellow and blue" suggests, is the character of the Swedish people. And it begins by attempting to explore, in a thoroughly anarchistic way, many of the questions that had been troubling me on the way to the movie house that night.

Sjoman begins by turning the camera on himself. Not only is he making a picture, a fictional narrative, but he wants the audience to understand that it is fictional, so he and his actors and the camera crew are constantly involved with and intruding upon the fictional action. The effort is to do away with pretense, but at the same time Sjoman and his crew become, as elements of the movie, fictional as well. Another level is the voice-over commentary by Sjoman and others, outside the visual action; still another is the fantasy life of the fictional heroine, which intrudes into the fictional narrative without warning or explanation and is treated in exactly the tone used for other, more "real" levels of consciousness.

The fictional heroine is played by Lena Nyman, a young actress who worked with Sjoman on an earlier film called *491* (which in its time had serious censorship troubles here too). When the film begins, she and Sjoman are having an affair, and at the same time working out plans and probable improvisations for a new film starring Lena. They evolve

164

a fictional Lena who goes about Stockholm with a microphone, asking people if they think Sweden has a classless
society. These sequences are all *cinéma-vérité,* and pre-
dictably the answers she gets are stupid, uninvolved, and
uncaring, this in a country where social concern is supposed
to be the first order of business. Fictional Lena then sees a
film about Martin Luther King, becomes obsessed with his
theories of nonviolence, and finds in her freewheeling inter-
views around town that people know even less about that
subject than they do about the class society. More and more
involved with issues she is only beginning to understand, she
turns her room into an "institute," collecting political pam-
phlets by the crate.

Fictional Lena has a rather pathetic father (who appears
only in the fictional context), whose one encounter with
idealism was a brief excursion to Spain during the Civil
War. She has never learned why he stayed only three
weeks; every day she totals the number of days since he
returned from Spain. His total lack of commitment to anything puzzles and disgusts her. It is then her bad luck to
fall in love, quite abruptly, with a boy who is no more committed to anything than her father is. It is with him that
the sexual scenes are played; a description of two such interludes may clarify what is happening in the kaleidoscope.

Lena and Borje (her lover) have spent most of a day and
night making love in her room. During a break, Lena takes
down vital statistics on Borje, explaining that she keeps a
kind of card file on her lovers, of whom he is number
twenty-four. At dawn, they go out on Lena's bicycle and
wind up at the Royal Palace. Straddling the balustrade in
front of the entrance, probably the most public place in
Stockholm, Borje gets the idea that this would be a good

spot for capping off the evening. Meanwhile, the camera gives us panoramic views of that whole area of Stockholm at dawn—the palace, the parliament building, the banks, the opera—while Lena's voice-over remarks in a silly-sweet singsong: "Now the Prime Minister gets up to take care of Sweden . . . and Torsten Eriksson gets up and makes pee-pee; and begins devising another defense of the new State Prison at Kumla." Suddenly we are back on the balustrade; Lena pulls her panties off, straddles Borje, and the pair start to rock cheerfully to a private rhythm, their only witness a startled, goggle-eyed guardsman at the palace entrance. It's a very funny moment in the film, believe it or not; and the political implications are unmistakable.

However, the sexual scenes that appear to have most disturbed U. S. Customs are those in which Lena and Borje are completely naked. These occur at a country cottage where Lena has gone to get away from Borje, whose infidelities have made her jealous and whose indifference to politics she finds maddening. Borje finds her; she waves him off with a shotgun. He snatches the gun away, throws Lena to the ground, and buries his head between her thighs. In the next scene both are naked on the grass, and Lena is lightly, lazily kissing Borje's penis. Subsequent scenes find them making love in a lake and out on a limb of the oldest, fattest tree in Europe. The idyll continues until one morning she taxes Borje once too often about the other women in his life; they have a screaming, shouting fight inside the cottage, while outside we see the embarrassed film crew trying not to hear too much. Back inside, Borje takes Lena, viciously, angrily, and then leaves her, apparently for good.

Suddenly, we are outside the cottage, and Lena has her

twenty-three former lovers tied to a tree. She is about to execute them with a submachine gun when Borje comes running toward her through the forest. Lena turns, mows him down, goes to the corpse, and castrates him with a knife. Immediately, we see Lena pedaling miserably back to Stockholm along a muddy road. Passing cars fling mud up on her; she is in despair. A car pulls up, moves slowly along beside her. The driver is Martin Luther King, and he wants to help her.

"Listen, Martin," says Lena, "I'm terribly sorry that I just can't make it when it really matters, but that's the way it is. He's a big shit, that Borje! A big fucking shit and I'll *kill* him when I get hold of him. I'll cut off his cock!" Shocked at her own passion, she pauses, recovers, and finally continues.

"You've said it yourself, haven't you? If you can't live by the principles of nonviolence, you shouldn't be in on it."

So Lena learns, the hard and only way, that it is possible to be hurt badly enough to want to kill; the audience learns the same lesson, less painfully of course, but not without shock. At the same time, through the breakdown of certain scenes in which Sjoman is seen directing Lena and Borje, it becomes apparent that Lena's affair with Sjoman is at an end, and she is now romantically involved with Borje. The point-counterpoint pattern is that, while the fictional relationship of the pair disintegrates, the "real" relationship flowers. The final scenes of the fictional relationship show the pair parting with anger and indifference. In "fact," quite the opposite has occurred.

Sjoman, increasingly rejected by his actors, professionally and personally, feigns indifference. When Lena comes to his cutting room to return the key to his apartment, he is sitting with another actress who is apparently going to be Next. Obviously, Sjoman isn't hurt a bit.

Or is he?

When Mr. Irving Fishman testified against *I Am Curious (Yellow)* at its obscenity trial, he told the court: "I felt that the dominant theme of the film was sex. The scene of sex intercourse on the floor of Lena's room, the scene of intercourse on the balustrade, the one in the tree, the one in the lake, the scene in the cottage—several scenes of fornication in the cottage, the scenes of fellatio, the scenes of cunnilingus—these helped me make up my mind rather quickly . . ."

Perhaps too quickly. No quick conclusions came to me, nor to my Australian companion. As we left the theater he lit a cigarette—rather testily, I thought—and strode along in silence for about a block. "Dammit," he finally said.

"What's the matter?" I asked.

"Well," he said. "It was supposed to be a sex movie. But it isn't about sex at all."

Okay, Mr. Irving Fishman. Put that in your customhouse and screen it.

encounter in london

yoko Ono is in the news a lot these days, because she married John Lennon of the Beatles, who is a
genuine Famous Person. That makes Yoko Ono a famous
person by association, which must be very entertaining for
her. Lately they enjoyed a rather populous honeymoon at
the Amsterdam Hilton, surrounded in their bed by reporters.
I know this hostelry well; it is well out of the center of
town, and very staid and Dutch, and though it is a Hilton
it is not a Howard Johnson's; it's very individual. I have

thought often lately of John and Yoko Lennon, freaking out in the Amsterdam Hilton, where I once spent a quiet weekend writing an Important Article. It doesn't scan; it doesn't scan at all.

I bring all this up because I know Yoko Ono slightly, very slightly indeed. But I did once meet her at a party which was probably more interesting to me than to her, since it was given for me and not for her, and I doubt if she ever knew or cared about *that*. But her fame by association has brought the recollection back to me—I live on the whole a pedestrian life, and do not meet many famous persons, and tend to remember it when I do.

It was a couple of years ago, and I was in London to do two Very Important Articles, neither of which was ever published. In any case, I was having a wonderful time by day and night, and disproving the arguments of all the London journalists, who like to write in American magazines that London is not a swinging town. London is an extremely swinging town if you have any idea what swinging means, and will do it. I will say now that London is the only town where I have ever been invited to an orgy in precisely those terms. "Oh, hello, Dick, we're so glad to hear you're in town. We're having an orgy on Sunday, can you come?" Those terms, exactly. So don't pay any attention to those journalists from London who are only looking to make a buck by denying what is so: London swings.

Anyway, I was busy accepting that kind of invitation and having a very good time, and spending quite a lot of time otherwise among the Elgin Marbles at the British Museum (I said I was doing two stories) when Yoko Ono came to town. I had heard of her somewhat in New York, where she and I had been living for some years at a considerable distance from one another, and nothing had ever compelled me to attend any of her events or brought us both together at a cocktail party or anything of the sort. But when she got to London everybody turned on at once to her, and the *Daily Telegraph* instantly ran a photograph of a segment of her gallery showing, and it all indicated that London is a smaller town than New York.

In her gallery show, Yoko Ono was at pains to delineate the basis of things, the home truth which was later expressed as the nitty-gritty of things, and the subject of the *Daily Telegraph* photo was a composition of three plinths, with a prophylactic device atop each plinth. As I recall, there was an antique netted sponge atop one, and a condom atop the next, and the Pill atop the third. I'm not sure—it's a while ago, she may have had other selections than those I list, but certainly the plinths were three and the third was as indicated. Naturally the London avante garde fell to pieces enthralled over this kind of thing—so clean, so crisp, such insight. Subsequently, Yoko Ono gave a concert performance which I only heard about. On this occasion she sat in the lotus position, center stage of the auditorium. The person seated first on the left in the front row came forward and received a whispered message from Yoko Ono. He then whispered this message to his neighbor, and so on through the auditorium, until the very last person on the far right in the last row of the balcony had received the message. You will remember this as a party game of our youth, the joke of which is that the original message gets so fantastically garbled in lengthy transmission.

Everybody thought that when the last person in the last

row had got the message, he would go up and whisper it to Yoko and she would announce it and the auditorium would marvel. But Yoko Ono didn't ask for a transmission of the message. She just smiled inscrutably and got up and went home. And everybody who had sat there for two and a half hours also went home, feeling very cross indeed. That was the nice thing about Yoko Ono; she always put a fresh twist on things.

Now I have a friend in London who is a fine critic and editor and he is a great friend and benefactor of the avant garde; that is the crowd he runs with, and he writes about them a great deal, and has done them all no end of good. Purely incidental to all these matters, he said to me one day that he meant to give me a party, to meet the crowd he runs with and to the end that we should all have a good time. And at great trouble to himself he arranged to throw such a party, and to have it in his own sumptuous London flat, which happens to be filled with the works of art of the very people he has so befriended. It is a remarkable flat for more reasons than that; he has, for example, a silver bathroom, which I am sure is the first silver bathroom in our time, though now there are many, and every two-for-a-penny interior designer is doing them, but he was first.

In any event, he threw the party, and it was certainly the most remarkable party I have ever attended. In the first place it was a terribly cold day—that is to say, a perfectly ordinary winter day in London to Londoners, but a freezing day to Americans. I had spent the bulk of that day with a curator of Romano-British antiquities at the British Museum, and we had been either in his office, which was vast and heated by a single-coil electric heater, or picking among his bone collection, which was housed in a room completely without heat, and I don't mind saying that by the time I got to that party, I was blue with cold.

My host greeted me warmly at the door, and hurried me toward the fireplace, where he had kindly laid down a very agreeable coal fire in the grate. Huddled as close to it as he could get was Martin Freedman, the director of the Walker Art Center in Minneapolis, whom I was astonished to see. I had interviewed him in Minneapolis two years before, for another Important Piece which was never published, and I scarcely thought to lay eyes on him again. Yet here he was, not so much to attend the party as to gossip with my host for a quick while before the party really began to exist, at which point he meant to make a speedy exit. So we chatted agreeably and jostled each other for a good position in front of the glowing coals, until the multitude of guests began to arrive and I had to come forth to shake hands with people.

Shortly I discovered that shaking hands was a ritual that could be dispensed with; nobody really wanted to do it, being English, and in any case quite indifferent to whom the party was being thrown for. The essential thing for them was to get a glass of cider and then to commence to discuss painters and sculptors about whom I hadn't a clue, and I spent all my time nodding and becking in a manner which I hoped would simulate interest and amazement. In course of time I was introduced to a lady who was said to be the mistress of a famous painter; "Oh, Dick," went the introduction, "have you met Sylvia, Reginald Roundelay's mistress?" She was a pretty American girl, and we got on at once; she asked me how I liked London, and I said I was freezing to death. "Oh, then," she said, "you must get proper underwear, knitted underwear, like mine." Saying which, she at once unbuttoned and displayed to me her underwear.

At about this point, the room quite filled with gossiping people and Martin Freedman long since departed, Yoko Ono and her husband of the moment made their entrance. It was a noisy one; Yoko Ono was fresh from a Happening in Trafalgar Square, and she had encountered resistance from some policemen there, and she was telling all about it. During the Happening, she had intended to drape the trees in Trafalgar Square with lengths of toilet paper, but the policemen had come up to her and said that they noted she had some toilet paper among her accouterments, and if she by chance had considered draping the trees with it, she should desist. Because if she *did* drape the trees with it, they would be obliged to ask her to accompany them to headquarters, and it would be terribly distressing to everybody. So Yoko, being no fool and not interested in accompanying any policemen anywhere, had concluded her Happening without introducing toilet paper, and instead had brought the lot, two cases of it, to my friend's flat. Very kindly she made a gift of it to our host, and signed each cardboard carton of it with a flourish, as a gesture of good will. He put the two cases in a corner of his drawing room and everybody was delighted with the gift and declared that the toilet paper was a Found Object and marvelous.

Toilet paper was not all that Yoko Ono brought to the party. For some while Yoko had been famous for advocating that everyone ought to get into black bags and take his clothes off and sit in there. She had even gone so far as to manufacture black bags and had brought a bunch along to the party which anyone might get into if they felt like it. The word was passed that Yoko Ono had brought these black bags along to enhance the party, but that if anyone wanted to keep one, it could be bought from Yoko for five guineas.

I was of no mind to buy a black bag for five guineas; certainly not something I could stitch together from a pair of old sheets by myself; but I was persuaded to get into one and see how it was in there. I had been watching other guests get in black bags, and the effects were quite remarkable. Here would be a group of three persons, nattering away to each other and sipping cider and smoking cigarettes like crazy, just as at any party. Then one person would slip this voluminous black bag over his head, from which he could see out and no one could see in. And before you knew it, the threesome would become a twosome. You just can't talk to anyone who's standing there obscured in a black bag.

Sure enough, I put on a black bag and it wasn't long before nobody was talking to me. You can't just walk over to a black bag and start talking. It might be somebody you know; or somebody you don't know; there's no orientation. But pretty soon my host brought over this other black bag. He said, "Dick, I'd like you to know Deborah Rogers, my literary agent." And I said, "By God, Deborah, I've been meaning to call you up." And we started talking away like mad, bag to bag. But we couldn't hear each other terribly well, so I sort of opened the bottom of my black bag and Deborah Rogers snuggled in, still in her black bag. And then we could hear each other quite well, and had a fine conversation, having a great deal in common in the way of clients and authors.

We also talked about the oddity of standing there in black bags, looking out on a room full of people who were ignoring us. All over the room were these looming shapes, these people in black bags, and nobody was talking to any of them. We concluded that black bags are the Great Answer to the awfulness of cocktail parties: you bring one along, and when things get inexpressibly boring, you put on your black bag and disappear, literally. You are physically present, nobody can say you snubbed the party, but you don't have to make conversation with anybody.

Deborah and I ultimately emerged from our bags for the best reason in the world. We had taken our drinks in, and had drunk them, and could have got more without coming out. But you can't smoke in a black bag; it wouldn't do; what a conflagration. After a while we both needed a cigarette badly, and there was nothing to do but come out of our bags and smoke cigarettes. For nonsmokers, however, of whom there is a growing number, black bags would present no social problem whatever.

Subsequent to our emergence, we talked a bit with Yoko Ono, who had not put on a black bag all night. She was a slight wee creature, and full of tiny alarms and exclamations, and great enthusiasms. She seemed very ingenuous and very pleasant; I liked her better than her poor husband, who was all tweed jacket and button-down collars, and had to carry all the bags, and was constantly nervous. He is well off without her, I suppose; no more hauling those bags around, anyway. Of course, Yoko Ono is not pushing those bags any more; she is closer to the basics now, and she and

John Lennon don't put a stitch between themselves and reality any more.

I like that; and I liked that party, and wish I went to more like it. It was the best party I've ever been to—and afterward my host and I went out to dinner and Tennessee Williams was sitting at the next table. I said it and I meant it: London is a swinging town if you know how to.

oh! calcutta!

oh! Calcutta! is still the hottest ticket in town—which, in New York, means that you have to buy your tickets months ahead at a very high cost (currently twenty-five dollars top) or, in order to see the play sooner, pay a scalper as much as forty-five dollars a single. *Oh! Calcutta!* is billed as an erotic entertainment. It was "devised" by Kenneth Tynan, consists of skits contributed by some of the finest playwrights in the country, and is played by a skilled and handsome cast who are, for most of the evening, stark naked.

So I was pretty pleased to be able to get a pair of tickets recently, and said so to my old friend the Establishment Critic, as I now call him. "Oh, well, I'm sorry for you," he said. "Sorry?" says I. "Why?" He looked at me with that prim smile, that narrow little mouth that is invariably affixed to the faces of New York critics these days, and said in a voice utterly weary, "Because, dear boy, it's *so* boring."

Boring, hell. I am thirty-five years old. Whether I am a sex maniac is debatable. But I have yet to be bored by the sight of beautiful naked bodies, least of all if they are deliberately bent upon entertaining me erotically. I am not immune to boredom. I have been bored by pretentious plays and pretentious people. And never more bored than by pretentious critics who try to mask their incompetence and embarrassment by hiding behind copout words like "boring."

Oh! Calcutta! is by no means an Important Evening in the Theater. It is nothing more than it set out to be—a minor, light-weight, entertaining Entertainment. And even such a reliably middle-dome source as *Time* magazine was moved to say that it was beautiful but *not* erotic. Surely that's enough to clear its reputation as an orgiastic sex accelerator.

Yet when my wife and I went down to the Eden Theater to see it, I did have the feeling that more than a few members of the audience were there on some dark and furtive mission. There was an indefinable air of Skulking About in the lobby. If you can describe anything so institutionally shapeless as an audience, I'd have to say that ours was . . . well . . . tacky. The point was made beforehand by a friend of ours who has a shop of imported Amazonian hand-

crafts directly across Second Avenue from the Eden. "Have
you *seen* the audience?" she asked us. And this from a lady
whose shop is only a few blocks from the speed freaks and
twenty-four-hour midnight of St. Mark's Place.

They were all dressed well enough, but they were not the
usual New York theater crowd. For one thing, they didn't
smell good, and a collective New York audience usually
smells ravishing. The only smell in the air at the Eden was
fear. And once inside the theater, there was a certain display
of unease, as if a lot of people there had not been in a
theater before. Certainly the occupants of the front row of
the orchestra were hardly a collection of theater patrons.
All male, these are the guys who pay the horrendous
scalpers' prices for the privilege of getting the closest gan-
der. A bunch of masturbation artists, they looked. I swear
one of them even brandished binoculars. And their tongues
were lolling before the lights came up.

Well, bad cess to them—*Oh! Calcutta!* just doesn't make
it in the masturbation department. It is lively and lighthearted, often beautiful, and consistently funny—though
some skits are distressingly reminiscent of the Princeton
Triangle Show at its corniest. The light mood and the
laughter seemed to puzzle much of the audience. Everybody
was ready for the opening number, in which the cast members line up across the apron and bump and grind their way
out of robes in a sexy satire of burlesque stripping. But
when the mood persisted, when heavy sex refused to rear its
heavy head and sexual hangups were played for laughs, I
detected in some of the audience a certain surly resentment.
Here was a bawdy presentation offered in a spirit not even
Chaucerian, but . . . omigod . . . relaxed. If I were a his-

torian of the theater, I would have to observe that *Oh! Calcutta!* has, like Kansas City, gone about as far as you can go, opening the field of eroticism to freer exploration by serious dramatists, excusing them from the dampening reviews that would otherwise charge them with exploitation by way of dam-breaking. *Oh! Calcutta!* has broken all the dams. Easily. The disappointed eroticists should have hastened down to the Gaiety Burlesk instead, for the heavy-handed stuff they obviously prefer.

By chance I know one of the stars of the Gaiety Burlesk. She is a girl named Vegas Carr, and I met her on the David Frost Show, where because I have written somewhat about nudism and nudity in the theater, I was one night invited to discuss such matters with experts like Vegas, who is a stripper. Now Vegas may take her clothes off with professional intent to arouse, and she may wear black eyelashes longer than her fingers, but she is a nice girl who aspires to finer things. Meanwhile, as she confided to me on that occasion, "a girl must earn a living."

On camera, Vegas said that she disapproved of nudity on the stage unless it was done, as she presumably does it, with beauty and good taste. Off camera she told me that she works five continuous shows a day and "the guys that come in . . . you should only see them . . . ugh." I asked Vegas if any old-time burlesque comics were working the Gaiety. "No," she said, "they feel that comics slow things down now, and the people don't come for jokes, they come for the girls." I asked her if that meant that there was no laughing in burlesque any more. She looked at me strangely. "Laugh!" she said. "You gotta be kidding."

Well, maybe the country has outgrown the broad, banana-skin comics of burlesque, and hasn't yet grown up to the aware, high-level amusement of *Oh! Calcutta!* Friends who've been on other nights haven't noticed the same tackiness in their audiences; it may be we hit a bad night, and I hope so, and am encouraged to learn that at other times the audience rises to the level of the production. We had a marvelous time, and felt very much in debt to a fine cast for our pleasure, and cross with the lady in front of us for persistently looking sideways away from center stage as if she couldn't bear to confront what was happening there.

The cast deserved her attention. Contrary to the general impression, actors do not take their clothes off in public any more easily than certified public accountants do. It took this cast many grueling weeks of work, not only in rehearsal but in personal encounter and sensitivity exercises, to achieve the freedom and effervescence they display on the stage. They work together brilliantly only because they have freed themselves to care for each other and, by projection, to care even for the jerkoffs drooling out there beyond the footlights.

The soundness of their success has had an immediate impact on the season, not only off Broadway but on Broadway as well. Hardly a play opens these days without the exposure of somebody's pubic parts, and if the play doesn't call for such a scene, we get it regardless. There is little value for the theater in this, but given the traditional cynicism of the business, nakedness for its own sake is a box office phenomenon we are just going to have to get through.

And certainly nakedness where it's needed, where it works, is here to stay. *Oh! Calcutta!* has done that trick. Some productions in need of nakedness even introduced it in the midst of their runs, shortly after *Oh! Calcutta!* opened. *Dionysus in 69* was one of these. The company had always worked *almost* naked, but there were jockstraps and stuff in use because of the police cars always parked outside the door. When I went down on a sentimental journey, not many days before the closing of the run, the police cars were absent from the street and the company was playing, at appropriate moments, completely naked. I was glad to see them freed of restraints that really made no sense in the context of scenes evoking Dionysian revelry and violence; and they are all beautiful in action, and I dug their bodies. But I had the troubling sense that they might be depending *too much* on their physical nakedness to convey the shock or sensuality that the particular scenes call for. By God, I think that when they weren't *really* naked, they worked harder at *seeming* naked. Which opinion may just go to prove that I have a lot more to learn about the theater. And about nakedness. And maybe, so do we all.

the first time I was ever in San Francisco, I was twenty-one years old, I was working for *Sports Illustrated,* and I happened to have the whole goddamn Hungarian Olympic team with me. It was at the end of a cross-country tour to raise money for Hungarian relief, and we were all physically exhausted and emotionally spent, and it was clearly time for a memorable party.

We had the party, all right. I don't remember much about it, but I do remember that it was in a suite of rooms at the Palace Hotel, and that I had a Hungarian Olympic saber in my hand, and fought a hell of a duel with somebody through the ornate rooms of that suite, in and out of mobs of drunken spectators, on and off the bedspreads and Duncan Phyfe furniture, flailing away like Douglas Fairbanks until the assistant publisher decided that enough was enough and separated me from my assailant, declaring both of us winners.

It was a right gesture in the right place, because everybody in San Francisco is a winner anyway, just by virtue of being there. And in what other town am I ever likely to fight a duel in a fancy hotel, without even a complaint from the management? And leave the party, and from a transom down the hall, hear Yehudi Menuhin practicing for a concert? What a great town for surprises, and a fine place for risks. In this case I don't mind making the simplistic assertion (something I'm prone to anyway) that San Francisco is where the good people live.

San Franciscans are lured into risk taking by the liberal climate of the city. But how did that climate come to be? I think the physical climate has everything to do with it—because when the weather is that gorgeous so much of the time, and guaranteed gorgeous only a few blocks away when not so hot where you specifically are, you are seduced into the confidence that the sun will certainly shine on you, somewhere near, whatever else happens. And the environment of a warm sun and silvery sea, gentle hills and gentler people—it liberates.

So maybe that is why all the best and riskiest experimentation with life, that current thrust toward openness in human relationships (that "new life styles" stuff people talk about), got its start in or around San Francisco, together with radical experiments in political and social action, in education, in psychology, and even in religion. Certainly since 1965 or so, in all areas of the human experience where change is rife because so warranted, the whole of the country has been taking its lessons from San Francisco's lead.

The thrust came initially from young people, of course, and the city is still a mecca for the very young, though the halcyon days of Haight-Ashbury and the power of flowers, in large part promoted by all the media in the country, are long over. The Haight, always ugly but for a brief time full of extravagance and fun, is now full of menace and fear. But the new style in living explored by many groups in San Francisco in the early days—all those wild and weird doings still conjured by the mere mention of Haight-Ashbury—has flourished widely, carried eastward from California on foot, motorcycle, car, bus, truck, film, and airwaves. This style still finds its fullest and most intense expression in northern California, and consists basically of at least four characteristics: the free use of drugs, principally marijuana; radical political action; sexual freedom and experimentation; and the expanded family and the commune. The formula which makes these characteristics possible can be encapsulated in one word, and it is an old San Francisco word: acceptance.

Because San Francisco is so open and accepting of experiment, this new style is in no sense "underground," as it may yet be elsewhere in the country. There is so much social and cultural cross-cutting in Bay Area behavior that the boundaries set by the nation's economic traditions simply don't apply. It is perfectly common for a middle-aged Pacific Heights matron to abandon her beige-and-white drawing room for an afternoon on the barricades at Berkeley or San Francisco State or the Federal Building, having made careful arrangements for bail in advance. This kind of living plays hell with the usual schedule of cocktail and dinner parties, of course, because the damnedest people wind up on the picket lines and in jail these days. But the damnedest people wind up at dinner parties, too. One woman who has been quite active with the Black Panthers was intrigued one evening when one of her dinner guests remarked that he had recently got out of jail. "What were you in for?" she inquired. "Rape," he replied.

This is not to suggest that all the barriers have fallen. There is the case, for example, of the wealthy doctor and his wife who wanted to know what this marijuana was all about, but didn't want their grass-smoking kids to find out about their experiment. So the doc got some grass from somebody down at the hospital, and very furtively he and his wife drove down to the Marina, parked, and lit up. Nothing. Huh! So they drove home grumpily, parked the car—and spent the next hour trying to get up the stairs, crashing, banging, reeling, saying sssssshhhhh to each other like a pair of bad vaudeville comedians. Of course, the kids still don't know that mommy and daddy turned on.

Although Ken Kesey's Merry Pranksters exist today only in Tom Wolfe's brilliant evocation of them, *The Electric Kool-Aid Acid Test,* the sort of tribal life they evolved has fired the imagination of many Californians, young or old, drug users or not. Most of the famous San Francisco rock groups are communal, and tribalization has come to the

Bay Area in an amazing number of forms. In many cases, the tribe may consist only of three people or two couples, and their children, bound together in loose economic ties or in thoroughgoing, total communality. There are tribes of single people, all straight, all gay, and even cross-sexual— one of these last having come about through the accident that all the members of it work for the same publishing company. Not many months ago, almost the entire staff of the *Berkeley Barb* defected from the publisher, banded themselves together, and started putting out a rival publication appropriately entitled the *Berkeley Tribe*.

Among most young people, a semblance of tribal fealty already automatically exists. The accidents here are that they are all young, all given to styles in hair and dress for which they are subject to random cruelties and threats, and all felons because they all buy, carry, and smoke marijuana. When so many thousands of people have a single felony in common, there exists a common fellowship which is almost religious in intensity. For many heads, in fact, the new life *is* the new religion; it has sacraments and rituals inextricably involved with sharing and openness to one another, and the confidence in a shared vision which often evokes parallels, they note, with the early Christians. The fervor of the young has excited the dormant hopes of many of their elders, and there is everywhere in San Francisco the sweet smell of burning grass, and the persistent notion that a new society is coming.

While that society continues en route, the city and its suburbs and its resorts provide the backdrops for all kinds of extraordinary human encounters.

A young painter I know had always wanted to visit San Francisco, but had put it off because he didn't have any friends there. Finally, when he got together a little money and time, he decided to go out alone and hope for the best. So he went to JFK and boarded TWA flight number 1, and was walking down the aisle of the plane with all his blond hair hanging out and his walrus mustache preceding him by a full inch, when this girl who was already seated handed him a copy of *Life*'s special issue on Woodstock. And he walked on to his seat.

So when they were airborne, he went up and sat with the girl who had handed him the magazine, and she dug into her Peruvian knitted shoulder bag and produced two joints, and they turned on there, high in the sky, and stayed stoned on grass and eight channels of stereophonic music, all the way to the City of Infinite Possibilities.

Later that day he was standing around in Union Square in the golden afternoon sunshine, contemplating the palm trees and the big TWA billboard on one side of the square, and the posh façade of the St. Francis Hotel on the other. The Hare Krishna gang were out in strength as usual, with their shaved pates and saffron robes, chanting and tinking their little finger cymbals and proselytizing among the multitudes. And this guy came up to him and they chatted amiably awhile and when it was clear that my friend was from New York and didn't have a place to stay yet, this guy purely *begged* him to come crash in his pad. "He's queer, he's queer," thought my friend. But the next thing this guy said was, "I'm not queer, no kidding. But I missed a chance to ask some other people to crash this morning;

another guy got to them first. So really, like . . . come on."

My friend did, and the guy had a groovy pad, and right away he broke out his stash and they smoked, and then there was a party to go to, and one thing led to another. And now my friend thinks he has more friends in San Francisco than he ever had in New York, and just may move.

The popular college professor, who loves the kids he teaches and is glad they feel free to drop in on him in the evenings, is nevertheless tired of being stolen from. "I finally realized that I'm just a patsy for lotsa these kids," he said. "Good for a drink or a meal or any kind of freeload, and what isn't nailed down they carry out when they leave—on the assumption, apparently, that they need it more than I do.

"The student body president needed a pad, and I let him use the old shack out back, and he lived there for three or four months. Then when he moved out, I suddenly couldn't find stuff—like sheets, blankets, an old jacket, canned goods. I couldn't figure it out for the longest time. And then I thought, 'Of course, stupid, he just took it. What's mine is his.' But hell, if he'd asked me, I'd have *given* him the stuff."

A student dropped by while we were talking. He helped himself to a cigarette from the open pack on the coffee table, then with exquisite nonchalance simply slipped the whole pack into his pocket. He chatted awhile longer, then, as nonchalantly, left. The college prof turned to me, his eyebrows twitching. "I assume you *saw* that," he said. And then got his coat on, to go out and buy some more cigarettes.

In an old, filthy, zinc-walled Italian joint on Broadway in North Beach, I sat with a bunch of people at a table by the plate-glass window. We ate salami and anchovy sandwiches on thick Italian bread, drank beer from little Pepsi-Cola glasses, and watched the world stroll by. The black hookers were in and out of the joint constantly in their shiny satin dresses and Marie Antoinette hairdos, working half the block, then checking in for a tiny beer, then moving on down their beat.

One of the kids with us, noticing that we were stared at by every pedestrian passing the window, began to wave familiarly at all passers-by. People wearing hip clothes never failed to wave back, to blow kisses, to flash V-for-victory signs. People in suits and ties and little mink stoles and Lane Bryant dresses were split about in half, some of the guys smiling and waving rather furtively, others flushing and hurrying past without another look. The hookers rewarded us with smirks; the only person to sneer and give us the finger was a U. S. Marine festooned with medals.

The hip kids hitchhike everywhere in northern California —every highway, secondary road, and country lane is lined with them. There is always a big contingent on the Marin County side of the Golden Gate Bridge, holding out signs for Navato, Stinson Beach, Mendocino, Oregon. Herb Caen reported recently that one afternoon, there was a kid there holding a sign that read HONOLULU. The local consensus was that he probably got the ride.

I was at a dinner party in Palo Alto, and after the steak

was consumed and the greasy dishes were cleared and every-one was on his second or third cognac, our hostess put on a record of African drums.

"I have *got* to do my famous African drum dance for you," she declared. And as the pounding commenced, she left the room and reappeared shortly wearing a sarong low-slung at the hips, a turban, and nothing else. I searched for surprise in the faces of my fellow guests but they just whooped and applauded and drank some more.

Well, the drumming was very intense and our hostess's dancing was damned exciting and the room got hotter and hotter and we were all fried out of our gourds. So pretty soon everyone was dancing, all ten good suburbanites (or reasonable facsimiles thereof), and it wasn't long before somebody shouted, "Let's all take our clothes off!"

So everybody did.

And then some neighbors dropped by, and they took *their* clothes off, and we were never even introduced. And at some drunken point my hostess was dancing on her dining room table, teetering naked up there, and she cried: "Atcheson! Catch me!" Whap! Down she came upon my concave chest, down we piled onto the carpet, knocking over as we fell a redwood magazine rack from which spilled, willy-nilly, latest issues of *Sunset Magazine* and *Saturday Review*.

It was early morning up on the coast highway near Men-docino, when I pulled into a little greasy spoon called Car-men's Casita for breakfast. It was just a shacky little place with a fantastic view of the ocean and a large parking yard, and the yard was full of California gypsies of every psychedelic description, and lots of vans and old beat-up trucks with Day-Glo colors all over them.

Carmen's lunch counter was small, and Carmen (presumably) was behind it, cooking up los huevos and el bacon and all sorts of stuff in a great flurry of activity. Her patrons were a Fish and Game officer, in uniform, eating snails; a girl drinking coffee and reading the score of *The Messiah;* a nervous, bearded gent in brown corduroy jacket, reading the brochure of the Evergreen Press; me; and on the far side a 1940's sort of lady with bright-red fingernails, reading the *National Observer.*

I was about to attack mis huevos when a gypsy girl in an army field jacket walked in the door and said in a loud voice: "Somebody in here got a picture of God?"

And while I was still trying to digest that, the 1940's lady looked up from her paper and said, "Why, yes. I do."

"Oh wow," said the girl. "Can I see it?"

And the lady dug in her purse and produced a tattered snapshot of some clouds and showed it to the girl, who said again, "Oh wow. That's far out."

"Yeah," said the 1940's lady, "it blasted me when I first saw it."

"Who told you to take the picture?" asked the girl.

"A little boy," said the lady.

"What was his name?" the girl asked.

"Jonathan."

"Oh wow!"

And I sat there, with a fork in one hand and a knife in the other, and wondered what the hell *that* had all been about.

I have a square old San Francisco friend who dresses in

square old Brooks Brothers suits and has a nifty wife and
3.2 children and all that necessary stuff, and makes it big
on Montgomery Street with expense account lunches and
belongs to the right clubs. So I was surprised when he remarked one day that I should come out and meet his neighbors. "Oh, yeah," he said, "I gotta expanded family on one
side—two couples and some young kids and some children,
and on the other side a homosexual couple. Been there for
years. We have cookouts and all. You should come."

"Ben," says I. "You are surely the most remarkable cube
in the world. Here you are so straight you can hardly sit
down, and you tell me about these kinky people living
around you without batting an eye."

He says, "Yeah, Dick, but you know . . . they're my
neighbors."

Downtown on Taylor and Ellis, its nearest neighbor the
Hilton Hotel, is the Glide Memorial Methodist Church.
Looks like any old up-tight downtown church, squatting
there full of Christian rectitude and flaking plaster. I expect
the Glide had all the problems of any urban church—lacked
relevance in the society of today, lacked even so much as a
residential core from which to establish a congregation. A
few little old ladies, lonely every Sunday in the vast sanctuary, organ music vibrating unattended in untenanted ma-
hogany pews.

Seven years ago a Methodist preacher by name of Lew
Durham got the call to the Glide. He had been working in
the Young Adult ministry of the United Methodist Church,
out in Nashville, Tennessee, and how the call ever came to
him I do not know, because by all appearances Lew is just

one of the Good-Ole-Boy network, one of those Bible Belt types you'd surely expect to snap his galluses if he thought the time was ripe.

But out he came to the City of Infinite Possibilities, and what should he find there but this empty church, and a perfectly good church hall, and a church office building housing the operations of the Methodist bishop, and some agencies of the Presbyterians as well, with plenty of room left over. And by pure coincidence a little extra called the Glide Foundation, containing six millions of dollars in funds expressly dedicated to the promulgation and promotion of evangelical Methodism in San Francisco.

Now Lew decided to take the widest possible interpretation of the Glide Foundation's franchise. So he put the money together with another simple equation, which is that the Church is the People is the Community is Us—and the extraordinary works of Glide got under way.

I heard about the Glide because a magazine editor friend of mine said, "You really must look into the Glide. I sent a girl reporter there to find out what they were doing, and the minister met her and took her down to what they call the playroom, and he dived into this huge pile of pillows and invited her to join him, and she wouldn't."

After that buildup I was determined to find out what these crazy Methodists were up to. It turns out that they're up to changing the world, these madmen. They're behaving like Christians, first ones *I* ever met, anyway. And they figure that the Church is not someplace where the Safe and the Cautious are to be stroked into satisfaction with their timid lot. They figure that the Church has got to be out in the society, working. So they have done this crazy thing:

they have identified themselves with the society *as they find it,* not judging it, just joining it.

This has led to scandal, of course. No barriers, whether of social acceptability or of dress or of sexual preference or of Christian commitment, limit the membership of the Glide Church. Christ, everybody shows up there of a Sunday. "I never read a rule," says Lew, "that the Church is supposed to inquire into what its members do in bed."

"Well," says I, "you weren't raised a Roman Catholic as I was, and didn't have to confess excessive masturbation every week."

"Well, no," says Lew.

One of the first things Glide got into was the homosexual thing. For a half-century San Francisco has been widely known as the Faggot Capital of the country, and what in the world are faggots to do about God, since in most churches there has always been a deafening silence on the subject. So the Glide established an ongoing study into the Church and the Homosexual, seeking out the Mattachine Society to work with. The result is a series of seminars designed at Glide which struggles to "demythologize" the homosexual experience, to expose professionals— priests, ministers, doctors, social workers, and interested laymen—to exactly what that experience is. The program is run by Ted McIlvenna, a Methodist minister who worked for a long time with the Kinsey Institute, and by Phyllis Lyon, one of the founders of the Daughters of Bilitis, America's first Lesbian pressure group.

Ted and Phyllis also have authority over the National Sex and Drug Forum, which strives to "demythologize" these two profoundly important societal fronts by means of encounter groups, exposure to a variety of mixed-media presentations of sex and drugs, and a large shot of Christian forbearance and acceptance. Not by accident, the Glide has become a sort of city switchboard of radical and disaffiliate groups, a center and a home where they can begin to talk to one another, to share problems and solutions. I tell you, these Christians can be sneaky.

There is a brand-new commune out on Pine Street, called Alternative Futures. Most of the members are seminarians, students at the ecumenical Graduate Theological Union in Berkeley. They have a little bit of dough from the Glide and a little bit from the college, and the seminarians will get a year's credit from living communally in this old church which is owned by the Glide.

When I was there, the commune had spent their first two weeks trying to make the old church livable. On the Friday evening, they were to begin a long vigil of silence and fasting, which they would not break until noon on Saturday. They hoped that in this period they would, through non-verbal encounter, come into the first stages of community. Alas, it didn't happen. I joined them at noon, and everybody (some twenty members, mostly young hairy seminarians, but including three or four middle-aged people—ministers, technicians) was stalking around in a diffuse and vaguely angry manner. Shortly they sat down to discuss what they had been through.

At first it was just an ugly rap about how some people had come to the vigil with *books,* and had sat there reading all night long. Big deal. Then there were a lot of personal recriminations, some of them very funny, about the impossibility of living in the conditions they were in. Said one girl: "I'd just like to know when my room is going to be My Room and not some goddamn corridor." Then somebody said they might best restate, individually, their reasons for being there in the first place, and for a long time everyone who spoke hid behind his or her doctoral dissertation or program or plan of study or Interest in the City. Until finally John Chu, already a minister and married to a neat girl and back in this commune situation for movingly personal reasons, the need for communality, said something about having always been on the periphery of life, having always deeply wanted the wider family, wishing right this moment that he could touch everyone in the room, out of his own need.

There was a leaping up, and embracing—first in the largest sense of group hand-holding, broken at once into small embraces, pairs and troikas and foursomes, and a gazing into one another's eyes, and a hugging and lifting and throwing about in the joy of contact. And suddenly it looked and sounded like a cocktail party in there, but the best cocktail party in the world—with no drinks at all, and everyone deeply, lovingly concerned with everyone else— and most certainly past time that they should all sit down and *eat* something.

Konstantin Berlandt used to be *Time*'s Berkeley stringer, and he was a fine reporter for such a young guy. He knew what was happening, and *Time*'s Berkeley coverage was consistently strong. But Konstantin has moved into something else now—the Gay Guerrillas, a group designed to bring the homosexual struggle to the streets. "I just couldn't take the journalism trip any more," Konstantin says. "I had to get into the Movement."

You might describe the Gay Guerrillas as a Maoist extension of the Gay Liberation Front, itself a far-left rebellion against the mild-mannered, Bingo-playing Society for Individual Rights (SIR), which in its time was a radical offshoot from the Mattachine Society.

The Gay Guerrillas are organized for street theater, for demonstrations, for teach-ins. They, and the Gay Liberation Front, of which they are a participating branch, are not doing any hiding this year. They are mostly very young guys, very much into the hip culture, and they are not interested in mollifying any up-tight straights; they want a revolution in the thinking of straights, they want an acceptance of themselves As They Are. They want to force confrontations and they feel that any other homosexual policy is simply dumb.

One recent Friday, the Gay Liberation Front threw a party at the Wesley Foundation Center in Berkeley (which happens to be owned by the Glide), and Konstantin invited me. I wanted to go in the worst way, but in line of duty I had got stoned that afternoon on somebody else's grass, and was lucky to get back to my hotel. However, Larry Littlejohn, the president of SIR, did go to the party. Although writers associated with the GLF call Larry a running dog of American capitalism, he was not afraid to go to their Social Occasion, and he said there were about five hundred beautiful cats there and he had a wonderful time. Konstantin talked to me on the phone afterward and deplored my absence. "It was beautiful," he said. "I felt a real sense of . . . well, like . . . brotherhood that night."

Considering how I feel about church stuff, I amazed myself one Sunday by turning out for the Glide Sunday-morning services. My companion, a thoroughgoing disaffiliate who keeps his hair in a ponytail and was at the time wearing a psychedelic velvet brocade vest and twill bell-bottoms, was even more amazed. "I Hate Churches," he kept grumbling as we drove into the city.

When we got there and tried to find a parking place, I remembered Herb Caen's aside that the Glide is the only church in the country where people are fighting to get in at eleven on a Sunday. We had to struggle for places in the balcony, so densely jammed was the main auditorium. It gave us a chance to look over the congregation, which is surely the strangest I've ever seen. There were, of a certainty, little old Methodist ladies with flowers in their hats, and little old Methodist gentlemen in black suits. There was, also, an abundance of wild flower people, girls in long trailing gowns, barefoot, working the amplifiers, and boys with cascading hair and blue-jean jackets, and Black Panthers looking awfully mean, and whole families of Ron Karenga devotees, even the littlest members decked out in leopard-skin shawls and electric-Afro hair styles. The world was present.

The interior of the church had been whitewashed, and a light show was playing, a sort of endocrine system of the soul, all over the walls and chandeliers. Where the altar must once have stood was a rock band, and little kids were sitting all over the sanctuary steps, and wandering around at will. The entire liturgy had been thrown out, and the

program spoke loosely of "times to" do various things—
reflect upon this or that, dedicate ourselves to this or that.
Lloyd Wake, one of the Glide ministers, made certain an-
nouncements and, when the announcement was popular,
was wildly applauded. One thing he remarked was that
Cecil (Cecil Williams, the resident black preacher) had
asked him to announce that anyone wishing to sing in a
group should drop by Cecil's house at seven on Thursday.
This message was relayed, in that folksy way, to more than
a thousand people, and I've wondered since how many
showed up.

The sermon was given by a lady named Laurel Glass,
who is the president of the San Francisco school board and
a member of the board of the Glide, and the two roles are
no accident, because the Glide was fully active in placing
Mrs. Glass on the school board. They have this absolutely
Machiavellian plan for putting good people into all kinds
of pivotal offices.

Mrs. Glass looks rather distressingly like Pat Nixon, and
comes over about as dynamically, and she managed to put
the whole church to sleep with her low-key address about
what propositions to vote for in upcoming elections. The
children were as restless as we ever were in my youth, when
bored to insensibility by the lusterless preachers who would
go on for hours about the promised intercessions of Our
Lady of Fatima. So I was glad when Mrs. Glass shut up and
we could get back to the light show and the rock group,
some profoundly direct praying ("We give our lives"), and
some community good times.

The services ended with the singing of "We Shall Over-
come"—which may not seem like much to others. But I had

never sung it with lots of people, and I was moved by every one of what seemed like eighteen thousand verses. We joined hands and swayed and sang, and the lighting experts managed to cast on the far wall a huge peace symbol, and the endocrine system swirled around it, and I felt . . . linked. I thank the Glide for that.

Pete Seeger was singing in the natural amphitheater atop Mount Tamalpais and we went. Six thousand other people did too, an unbelievable mob, so our ascent to the mountaintop was very slow. Not that we minded; it was a glorious day, with clear white sunlight, not a trace of fog or chill, and an unusual clarity to the edges of all shapes. Driving slowly up the twisting road, we admired the fuzzy brown foothills that tumble like giant nudes away from Tam's peak.

Of course we had terrible trouble finding a place to park, and had a long hike after that, hastening along paths padded with pine needles, and through avenues of sweet eucalyptus, until we came to the gate and went in among the thousands and searched for seats. Seeger just stood there under the cedars, practically swamped by the throng, and in his quiet way sang the songs that have moved people, at various points in time, to so many revolutionary or loving acts. There were some Day-Glo crazies behind the microphone who danced in a ring to every song sung; there were children around the singer's feet who cried requests, at every pause, for funny children's songs like "My Mommy said not to Put Beans in My Ears."

A friend I was with saw some of his students on the far side of the amphitheater, stripped to the waist, being terribly bronzed Californian youths, smoking grass and laughing and having a good time. "We could probably get some grass from them," my friend said. But we didn't act on it.

It was a hot sun and we were close to it, and the crowd sweltered in the sweet-smelling heat, and in course of time we all came together. People started singing along with Seeger, and finally the whole crowd was singing the lyrics of everything. At intermission a drum group came on, and various isolated people in the audience got up and danced by themselves and didn't mind if people on either side didn't dance, and the people not dancing didn't seem to mind the people who did.

At the end of the concert, half the crowd was weeping with pleasure and sentiment, and everybody was singing, and down our row I noticed soap bubbles rising from somebody's pipe, round and glistening with the sunlight and the green of the trees. Just in front of me, a family was sitting, and they had brought their picnic lunch in a cardboard carton. On the lid of the carton, someone had scrawled, in crayon: BE GENTLE.

And we were.

for a long time I kept a promise to myself
that I would not write about Monhegan, because it was one
of the best times in my life, and I wanted to keep it exclusively mine. The thing is that writers never get to stop
working, the way other people do. Even when they are just
sitting around dully drinking or something, a chance event
or a random thought can set them to work again, at once—
if not at once on paper, at once in their heads. It gets to
seem, sometimes, as if there are no experiences that are just

for their own sake; just for you. And everything in life becomes . . . material.

Sometimes I think we are as cynical, in our discreet way,
as news photographers, who never fail to photograph the
accident before going to the aid of the victims. The authen-
ticity of our involvement in events, in our very lives, is
altered and often warped, by the habits of the profession.
So when Jean and I went up to Monhegan Island for a week
a couple of summers ago, I swore in advance that I would
not function like an audiovisual taping device. I swore that
I would just *be* there. It didn't work, of course; I was writing the story in my head all the while I was living it, and
I admit that I may never be able to sort out the real distinctions between me the writer and me the human being.

And now I feel that this book is the right place for the
story I was writing silently anyhow. So here goes—not that
there is any compelling story line that is about to emerge.
The problem here is that I will have to talk about nonverbal
experiences, and the hell is that words are, quite obviously,
not the appropriate medium for conveying what happened.
So I have to say in advance that if you ever really want to
understand what I'm talking about, you'll just have to go
up to Monhegan, and feel.

Monhegan is an island in the Atlantic Ocean, ten miles
off the coast of Maine. It is quite tiny, and most of it is a
nature preserve, though there is a minute fishing village on
the landward side. Birdwatchers and butterfly collectors and
little old ladies who paint have been going out to Monhegan
in the summers for many years, but it has never got very
crowded there because there is absolutely nothing to do but

live with nature, and that is something most Americans don't care much about.

For several years now, Charlotte Selver and Charles Brooks have spent their summers at Monhegan, giving classes in sensory awareness. I don't suppose *they'd* call it that; being not very verbal on purpose, they'd probably prefer not to call it anything. Classes in being might be more accurate; on rare occasions Charlotte and Charles have been heard to call it "the work." Whatever it is, I badly wanted my wife and me to have some of it. I had met Charlotte and Charles at Esalen, but hadn't worked with them; others reported with eyes glowing that we *had* to go to Monhegan, *had* to work with them, that the experience was extraordinary. Jean, resentful at not having had the Esalen experience which had so wrenched our lives, understandably apprehensive at what she might be *made to do* at Monhegan, nevertheless agreed to go to Monhegan and see.

The trip alone was good fun for us. We both love Maine, and it was lifting just to drive into Boothbay Harbor, and find a week's parking for the car behind the firehouse, and board the Sunday-afternoon ferry for the long haul out to the island. We had a gorgeous ride in the crisp, Maine-summer sunlight, over calm waters, through a wisp or two of tentative fog, out into the Atlantic.

From portside, Monhegan didn't look terribly special. There were the requisite gulls, standing around on the requisite rotting piers, and a few isolated, starkly white frame houses poking up from the rising slopes. The spareness, the slight sense of pinched, parsimonious planning, was richly compensated for by the brilliance of the field flowers, the high waving grasses, the forest greens, and the clear-lighted warmth of a fleeting summer. And, of course, there was the omnipresent sight and smell of the sea.

Monhegan House, the ancient but sturdy inn where we had booked a room, was run by a polite but no-nonsense lady named Mrs. Nicholson, whom we found in a rocking chair in the parlor-lobby of her establishment—a position of vantage from which she rarely stirred. We had from her an adequate room which was swept every day. The bathrooms were down the hall and the rates were very cheap. We were satisfied and so was Mrs. Nicholson.

Our week's classes were conducted by Charles, assisted by Charlotte. They were held in a white one-room schoolhouse on a knoll at the far end of the village from Monhegan House, and we walked there every morning to begin the day's sessions. After the first morning, we always took the walk in silence, that having been one of Charles's earliest suggestions. But at the beginning we were all quite chatty. There were about twenty participants, and we were quite a mixed bag. There were young students, there were yoga enthusiasts, there was a salesman, and there was a lady physiotherapist. There was a minister's wife. There was a singer. There was even a woman who'd missed out on a trip to Europe, and had come off to Monhegan with a friend on the spur, in a fit of pique. And of course there was Charles, sitting on the floor at the head of the room, suggesting that we spread our blankets and sit down and "come to quiet."

In the next days we "came to" many things at Charles's suggestion—not least of which the realization that our bodies were tied in dumb knots we didn't even know about. We learned to realize ourselves more fully than would ever have occurred to us independently, simply by means of coming to some awareness of the space each of us occupied—our real dimensions ("See if you can feel how far it is from the top of your head to the place where you come into contact with whatever is holding you up") and our real environment ("Are you standing on the floor, or is the floor supporting you?"). We also came to sense what was happening to each other, and by means of the gentlest touching experiences recognize the pain or tension that was present in somebody else's limbs, and have our own pains and tensions articulated to us by others.

And above all other things, we were quiet. Or at least we tried to be. I remember one afternoon, some days after we started, when the class was together on the high cliffs on the Atlantic side of the island. Charles had suggested that each of us select and try to *be with* some inanimate object in nature—a tree, the sea, the wind, anything. We would experiment with that for five minutes or so, trying to allow only the fact of the thing we picked, seeing how much we could partake of its nature. I had been standing barefoot on a large rock, and had noticed that though the day was grey, the rock was still warm from earlier sun. That intrigued me, so I picked the rock, sat on it, and tried to be with it. Hah. I could be anyplace else but there. My head felt like a bucket of garbage, full of shards and tiny bits of impressions from anything but where I was and what I was doing. All kinds of unnecessary information rattled through, and I found myself thinking of my mother, my dog, my car, my job, the wind, God knows what-all. Finally, I said over and over to myself, the rock, the rock, the rockRock ROCKROCK-ROCKROCK. And that did blot out most other things. But of course what I had done was to substitute a word for the quality of rockness, which I had missed altogether. And I thought, what a jangling, distracted, rattle-bang tin man I am.

Later we moved off the rocks into a glade, noticing (at Charles's suggestion) the difference between the hardness of the rocks and the softness of the thick grass. He suggested that we move about in the glade for a while, feeling what supported us; and then he made a really extraordinary suggestion. He proposed that we try to see without looking. The argument is that we are always probing and selecting with our eyes—we pick out of the general vision a red this and a textured that. Try, he said, not to select. Instead of probing, let your eye rest, and allow what comes to it to come. So we tried both experiences at once, feeling what supported us and seeing without looking, and I noticed that I was seeing more color over a wider space than is usual for me, and that I liked that experience very much. And then, while we were moving about in this curious way, Charles suggested that as we passed one another and if we wished to do so, we might reach out to touch each other.

That began very timidly, of course. Naturally none of us were unaware that we were standing like so many zombies in the middle of a public field, that passing lady bird watchers would be astonished to stumble upon us, that not only does one not do that sort of thing, one certainly doesn't compound the doing by *touching* and *being touched*. But most of us were on our way to being beyond that sort of tremor by now, and the early, tentative, short-lived touches became firmer, longer of duration, infinitely more meaningful. Because I was not selecting with my eyes, I was never entirely sure who I was touching, or who was touching me. That ceased to be important—but the variety in the intensity or warmth of other hands amazed and delighted me. I sensed that my excitement and pleasure in this experience was shared by many, that what had begun in random touching had become an entanglement of embraces, that in a physical but uncommitted way we were answering each other's needs as human beings. We were being loving with one another. We loved—finally, in an embrace that involved all twenty of us, holding one another silently in the warm grass.

And when Charles broke what had been unquestionably a magic spell, and we all sat down in the grass to "report" on what we had experienced, there were a few of us there who were too moved to speak. When we left to return to the village, three or four lingered behind, hoping to stay with the experience as long as possible. And one girl remained in the glade, weeping with relief and happiness, until dusk.

We had, after all, not really done anything so extraordinary. As Charles later remarked, a bunch of Tahitians or Trobriand Islanders would have thought we were crazy to need such a release—but the people of those simpler societies have never had to cope with the touch-tabu that so tyrannizes us. Is there, in fact, any reason why we should hold ourselves back so from touching our fellow man? And what have we done to our bodies in the constant, unthinking discipline of avoidance? And what have we done to our sphincters and our faces and our eyes? You would think we would all crack to pieces from the strain. We had already proved that we had not allowed nature to enter our consciousness in any significant way; finally we proved that we were fending off each other, even more formidably.

What we learned had verifiable, visible effects on many of us. I remember one girl who started the week in a terrible state. She was one of those nervous, awkward young creatures who can't talk without stammering, who can't walk without tripping, who can't sit without fidgeting, who can't eat without spilling. A disaster area. By the end of the week the girl had taken on an entirely new shape. She was quiet, she knew repose, she was even pretty. It was a miracle— and for her sake, I hope it lasted.

I don't know quite what to say about the long-range effects of this kind of experience. I do know that while it lasted it was supremely happy and liberating for all of us, and that when the first ferry pulled out on the final day, there was the goddamnedest farewell scene I've ever witnessed, between those of us who were staying on and those who had to leave at once. Not in Greece, not in Italy would you see any more weeping and embracing, any more hand holding and gift giving and kissing and waving. How a bunch of strangers could have got so high on one another in a week's time is still a mystery to me—except that I know that Charlotte and Charles assisted us to open ourselves to each other, and we did that, and it was a warmer and sweeter and infinitely more enriching experience than any of us had ever had or imagined could be possible.

It sometimes seems that the Monhegan experience didn't last for Jean and me any further than the end of the ferry boat ride back to Boothbay Harbor. Not five minutes later we were bickering over routes and luggage and plans, and a passer-by would have been sure we didn't like each other a bit. I guess we didn't, at that moment; but we did love each other a lot, and the confirmation of that does seem to linger on and is renewed from time to time.

This summer some friends of ours who had heard about Monhegan from us decided to go themselves. And after they had been with Charlotte and Charles for ten days, and after they had settled back in for some weeks in Boston, they loaded the kids in the car one Thursday and drove down to Princeton to spend the weekend with us. Out of the shared experience of Monhegan, our weekend began at a level of intimacy that we had never had with one another before. It had many dynamics, going from good to bad to awful to terrific to okay to sensational—which sounds exhausting, and sometimes is, but is worth it for the intoxication that comes with honesty and with being present for everything.

On the Sunday afternoon of their visit, we were out in the garden doing some Esalen and Selver-Brooks experiences—falling to one another, doing the backs—a whole bag of adult games built on touching. The children, theirs and ours, came around the corner of the house and watched us with some annoyance, because there we were, grownups, *playing*. I'm not sure it suited their idea of how parents ought to behave. But ultimately they started falling and carrying on, just like us, and then we were all being children together.

At some point I said I'd go in to fix the drinks, and Jean said, "No, darling, I'll go fix the drinks," and our friends said, each in turn, "No, Dick, *I'll* go fix the drinks." We were standing at the time in a circle, in a four-way embrace, which had come about through no particular design; and out of some general, unspoken assent, we *all* began to go in to fix the drinks, moving in our four-way embrace like some lumbering eight-legged spider, laughing at the awkwardness of it but learning, in the doing, how to move more efficiently. Believe me, the steps were tough, but we made it—and we found that, by being watchful of each other and by putting a little spin on the big embrace, four people can get through a narrow door just fine.